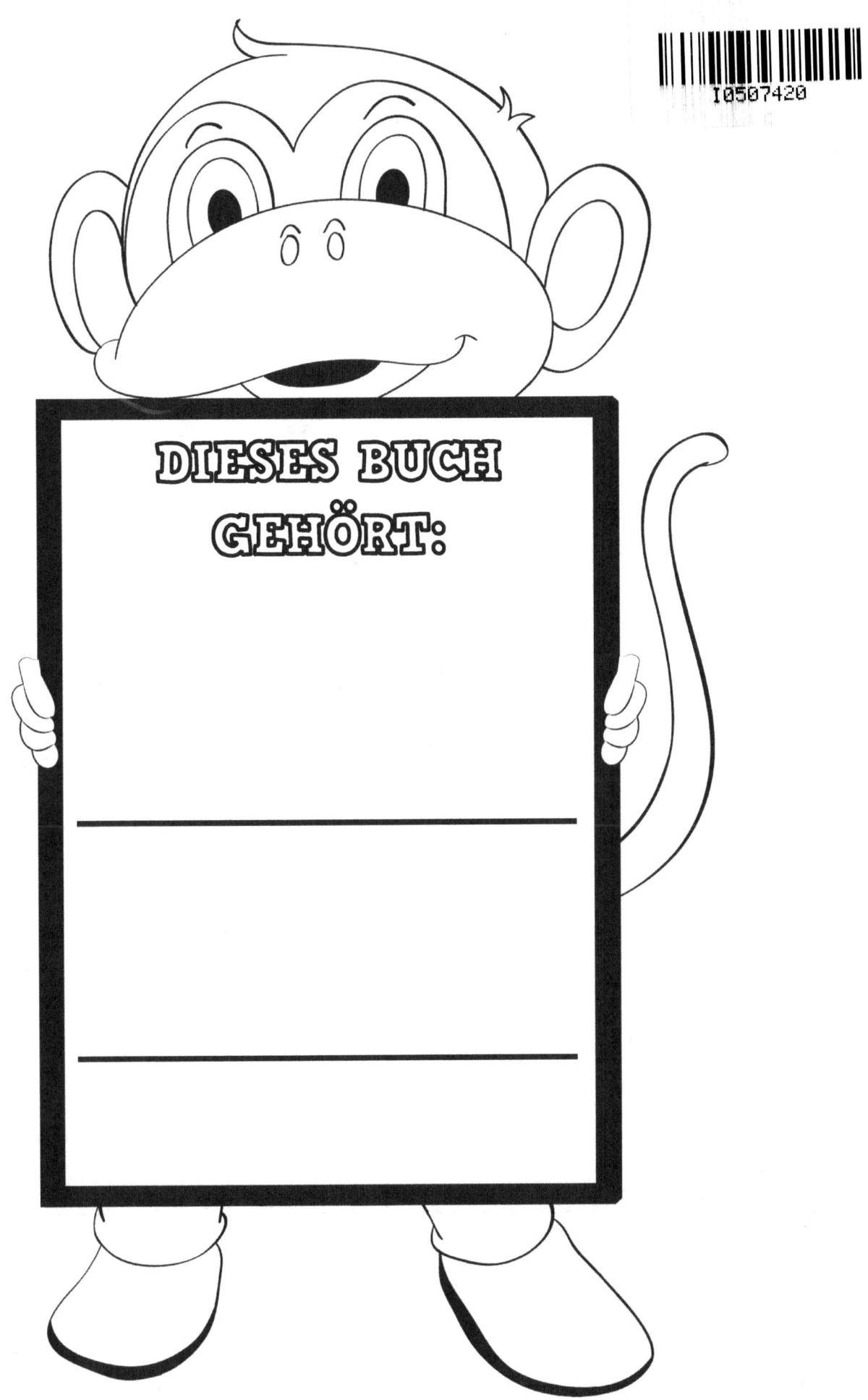

Ameise

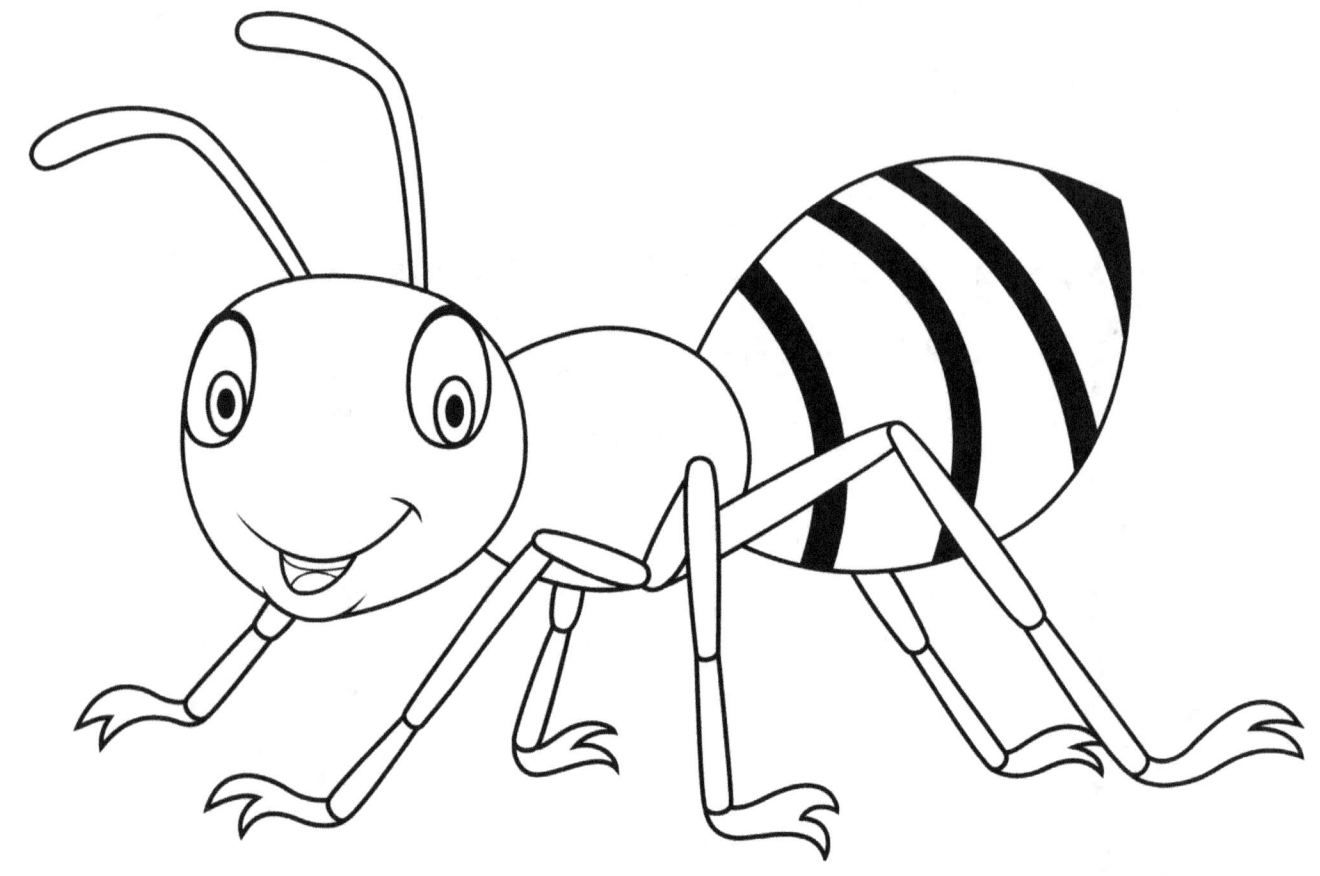

Ant

Ant
_____

_____

_____

Apfel

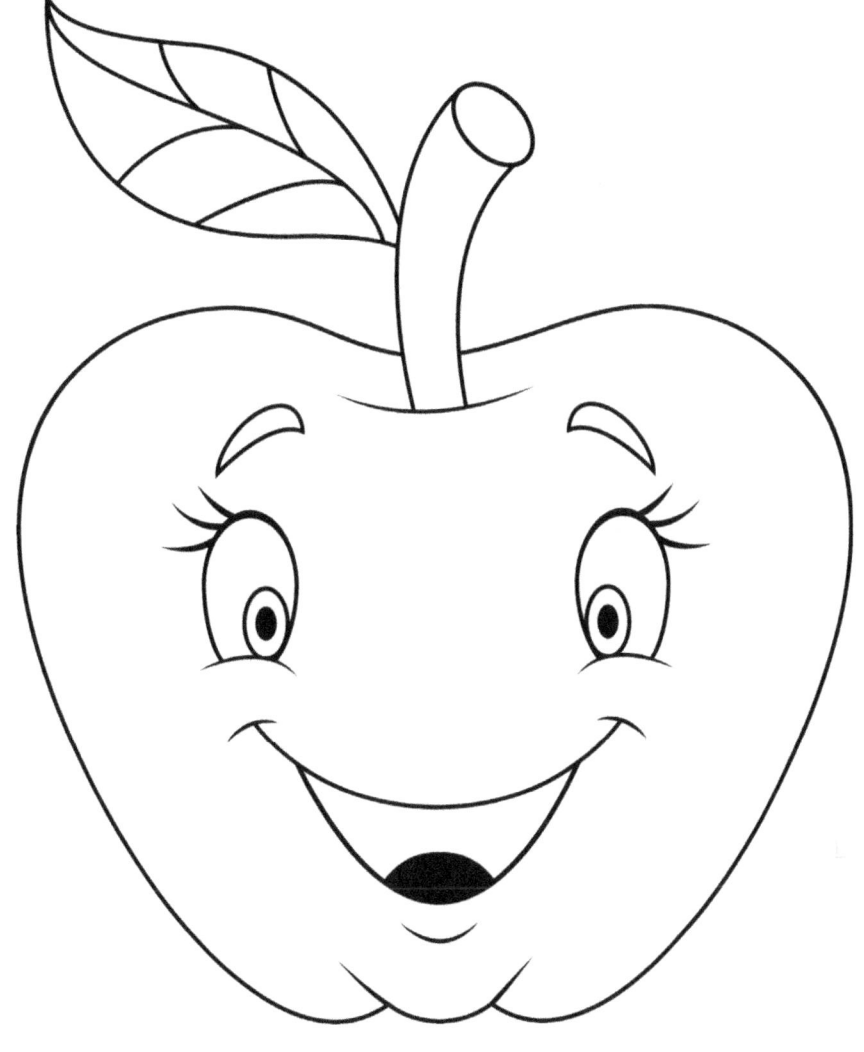

Apple

Apple

Raumfahrer

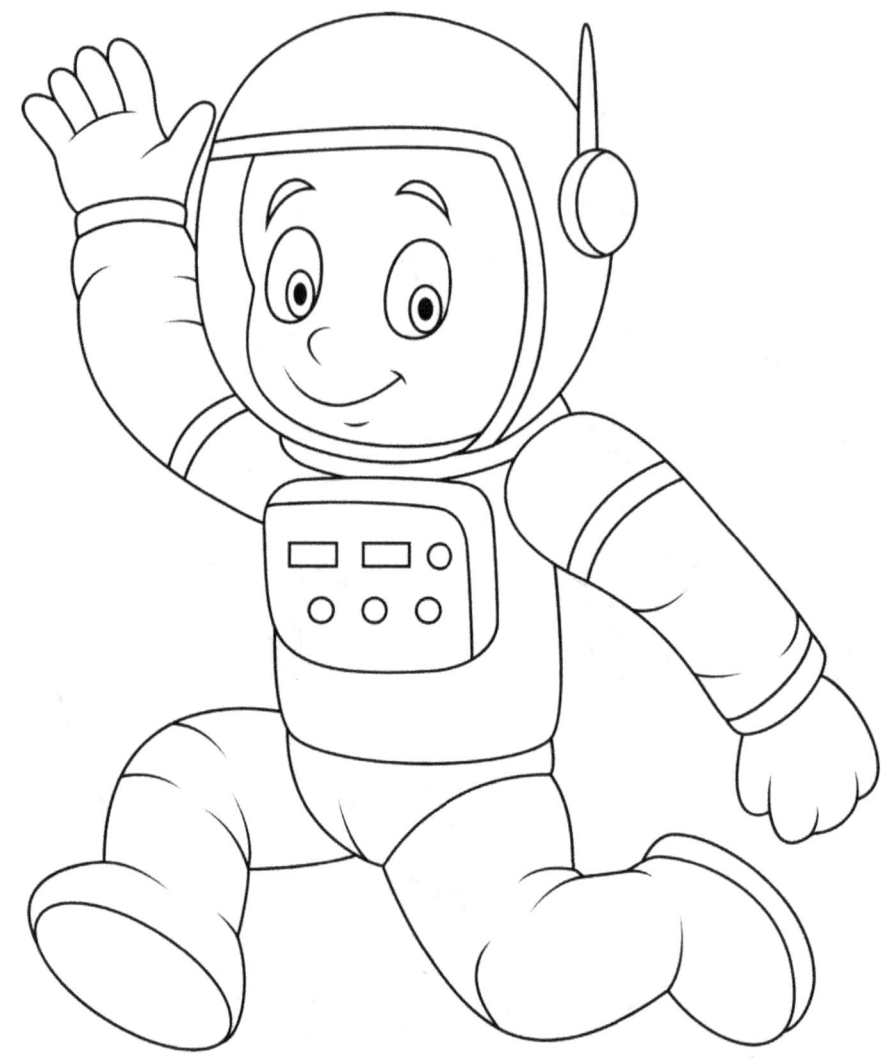

Astronaut

Astronaut

Banane

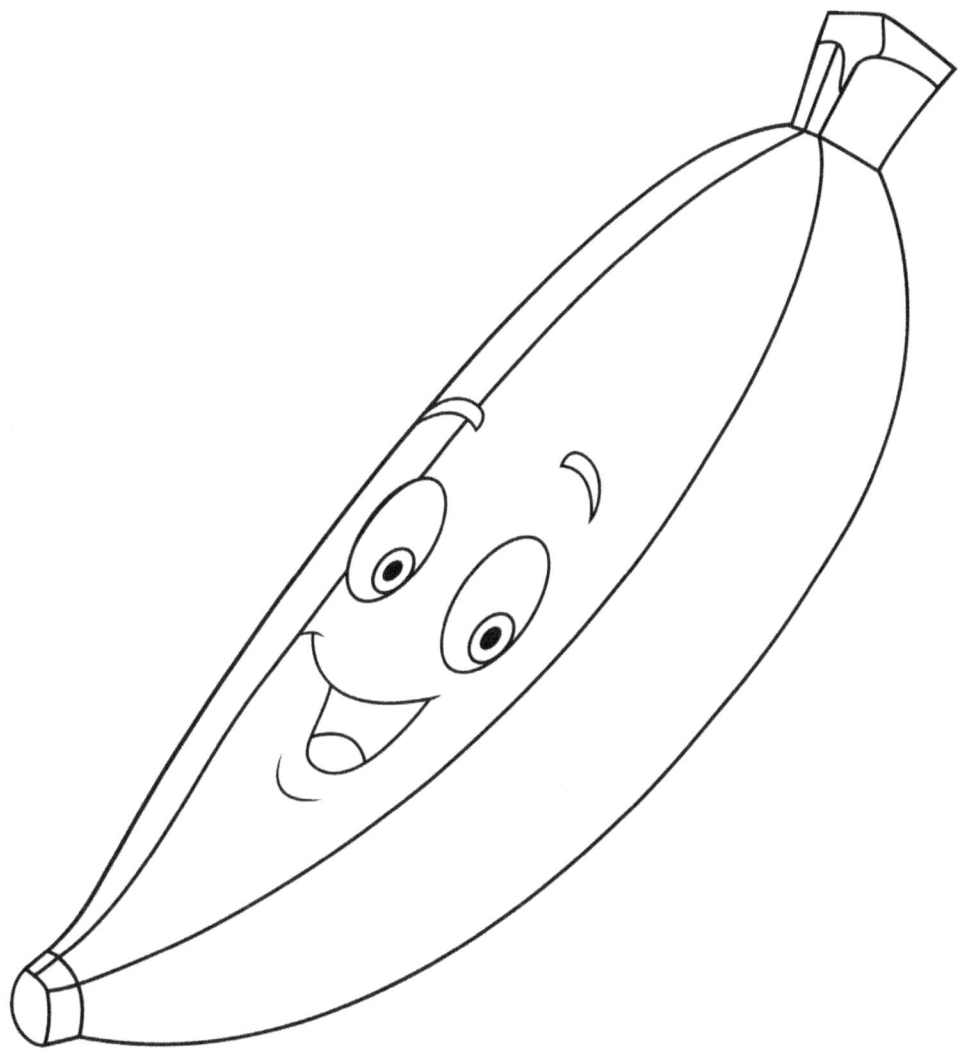

Banana

Banana

Ameise

_nt

Apfel

A_p_e

Raumfahrer

Astro_aut

Banane

B_nan_

Bär

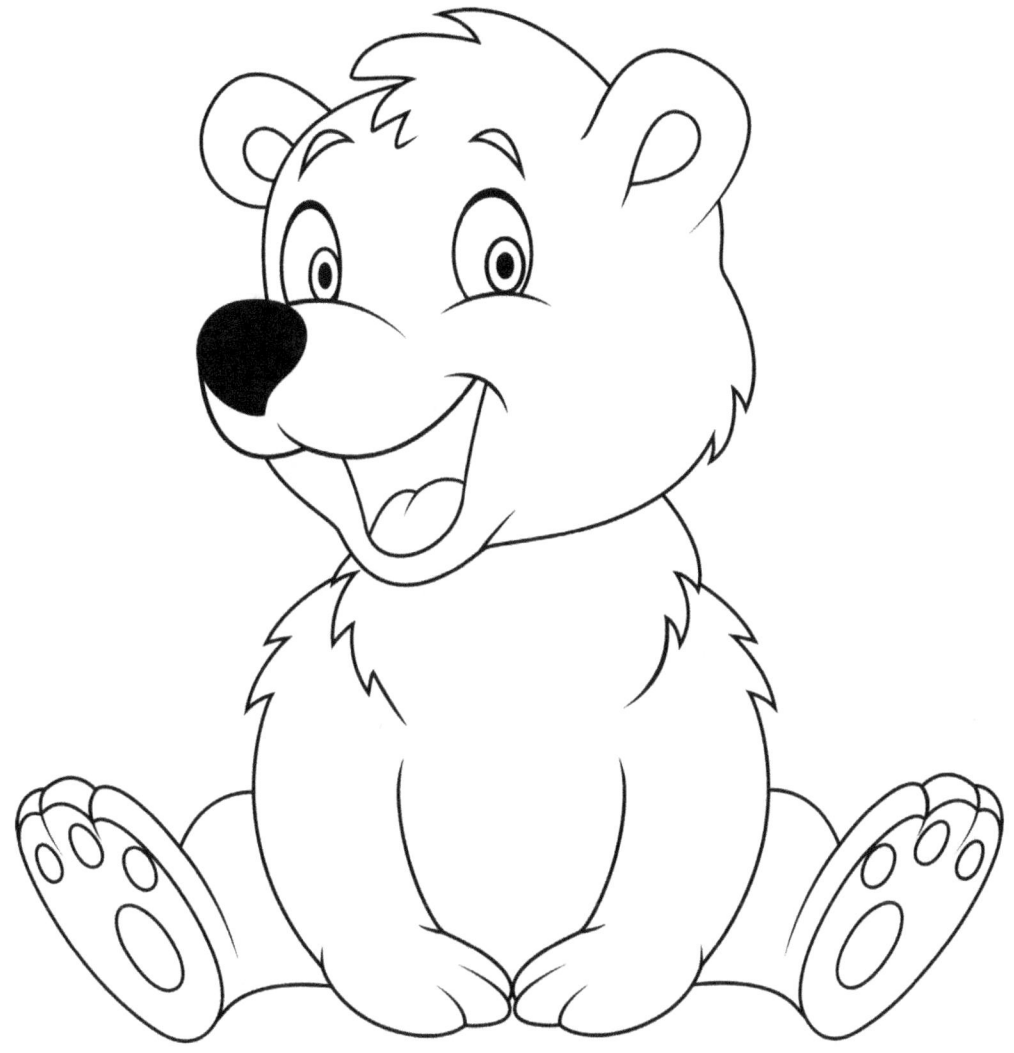

Bear

Bear

Buch

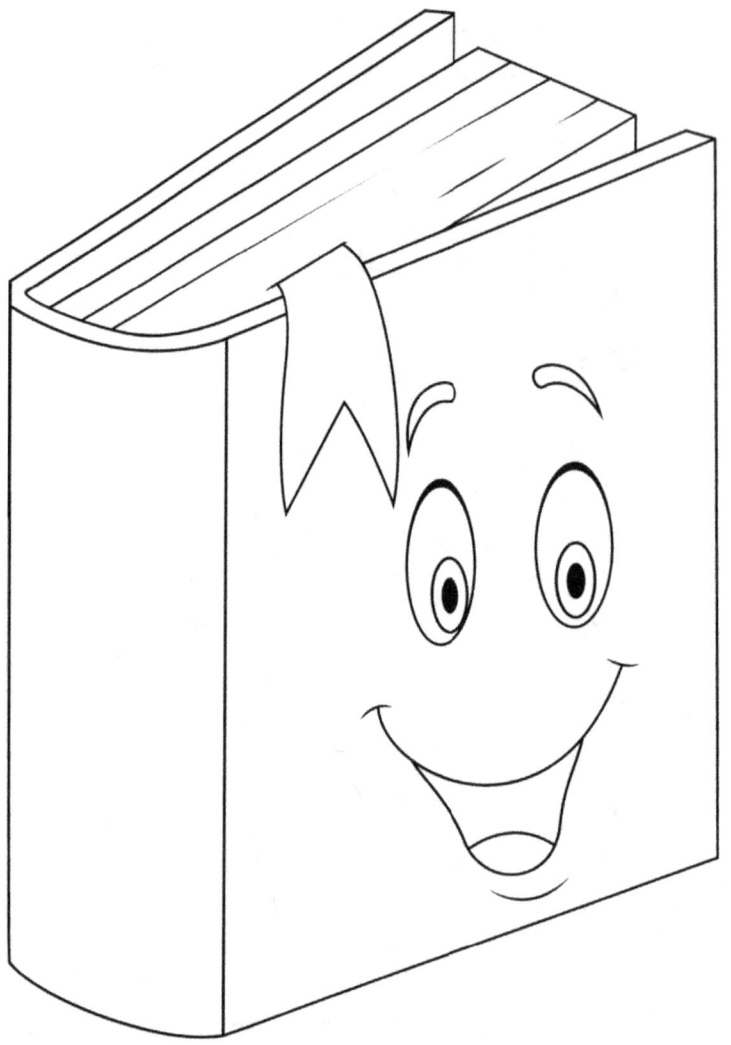

Book

Book
_____

_____

_____

Auto

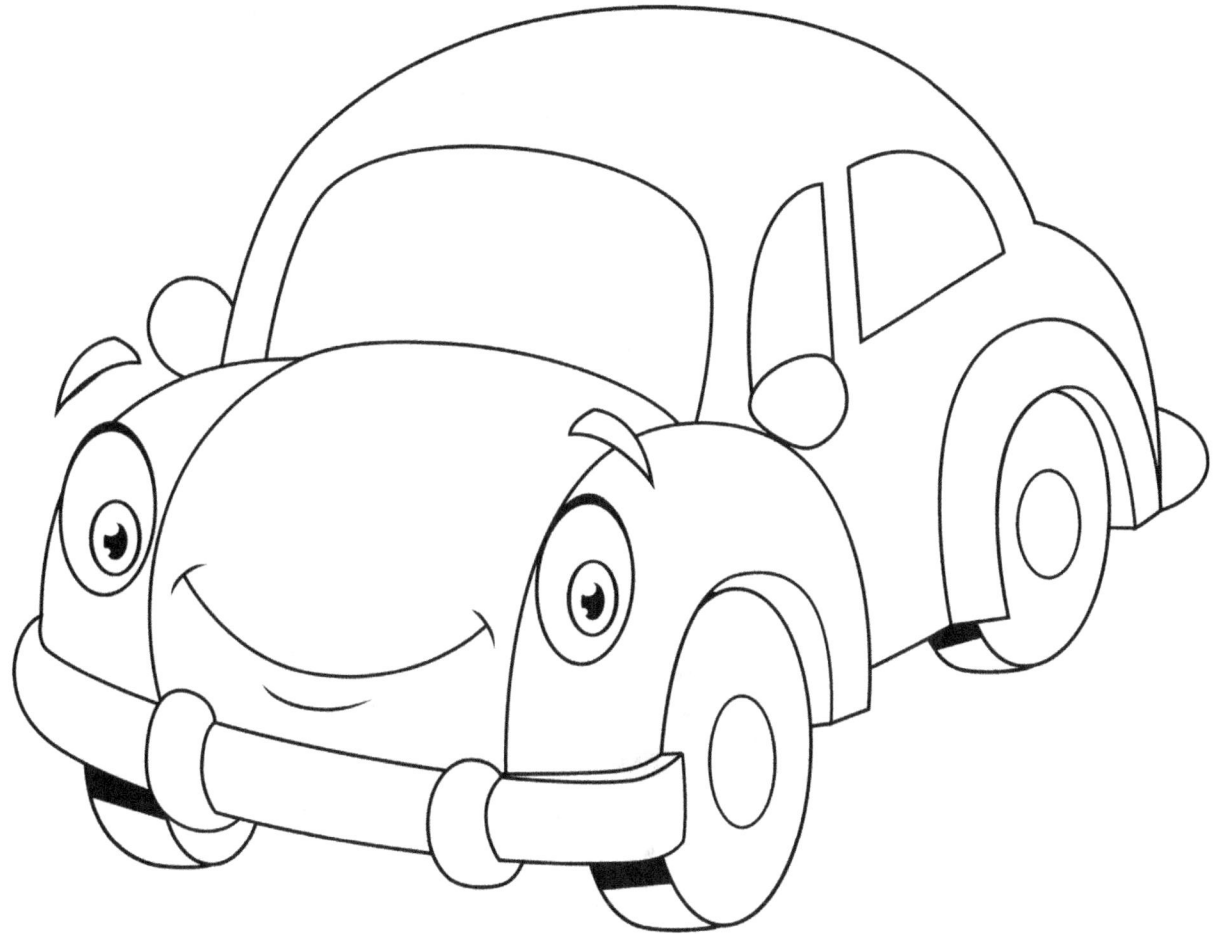

Car

Car
_____
_____
_____

Katze

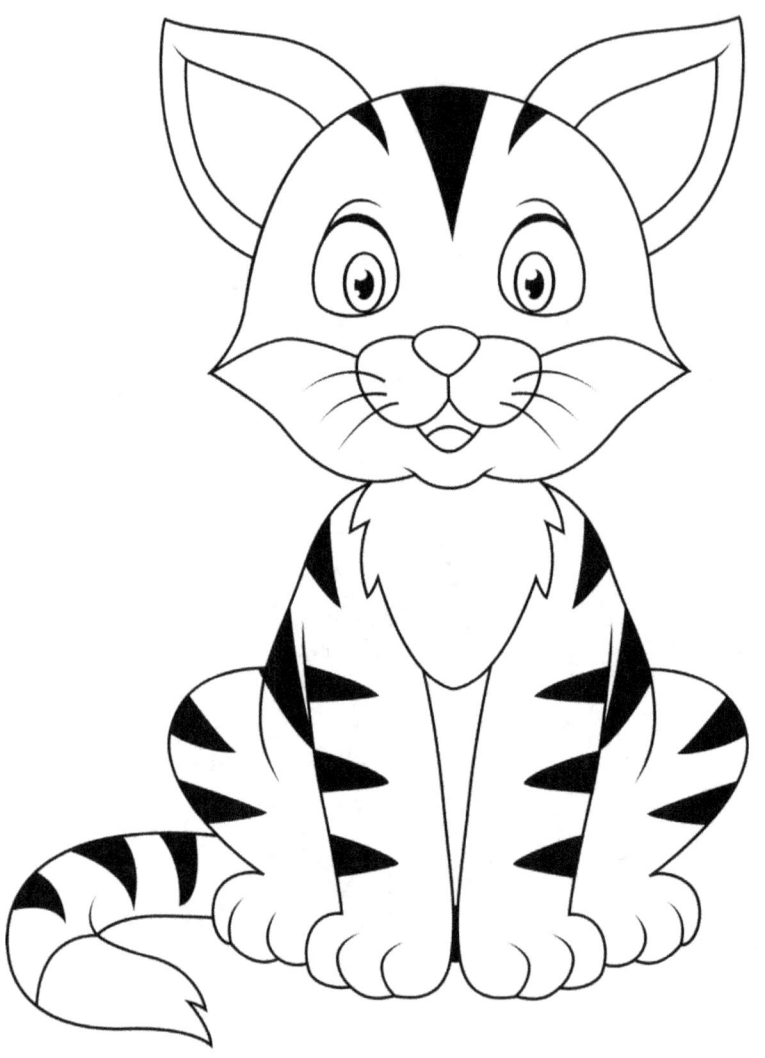

Cat

Cat

Bär	
	B_ar

Buch	
	B__k

Auto	
	_ar

Katze	
	Ca_

Mais

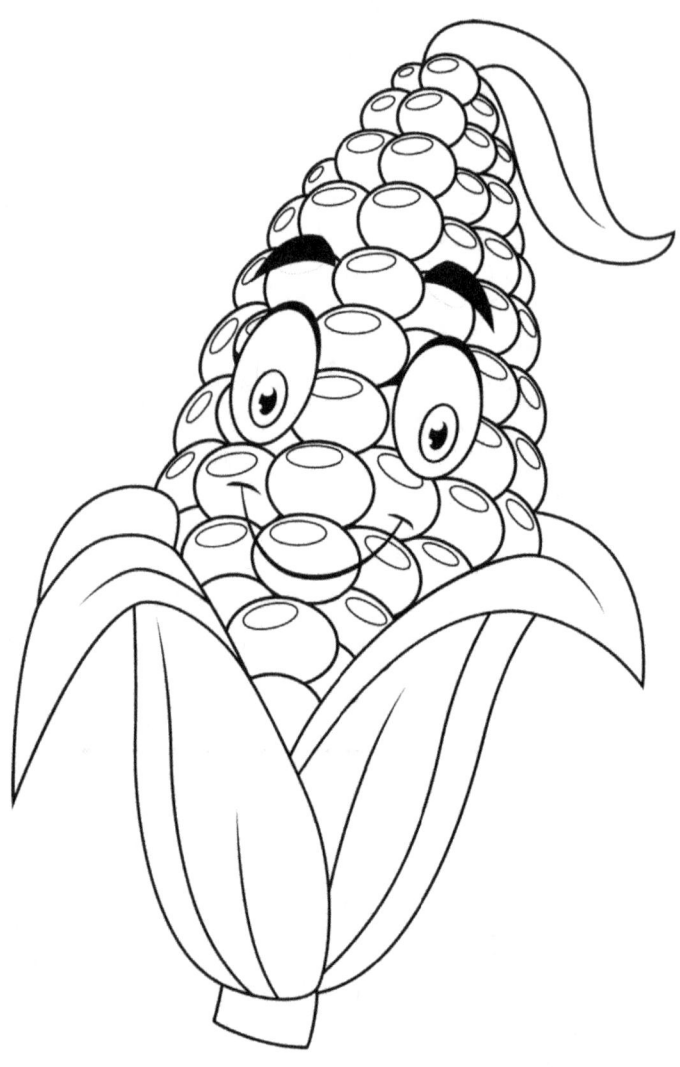

Corn

Corn

Hund

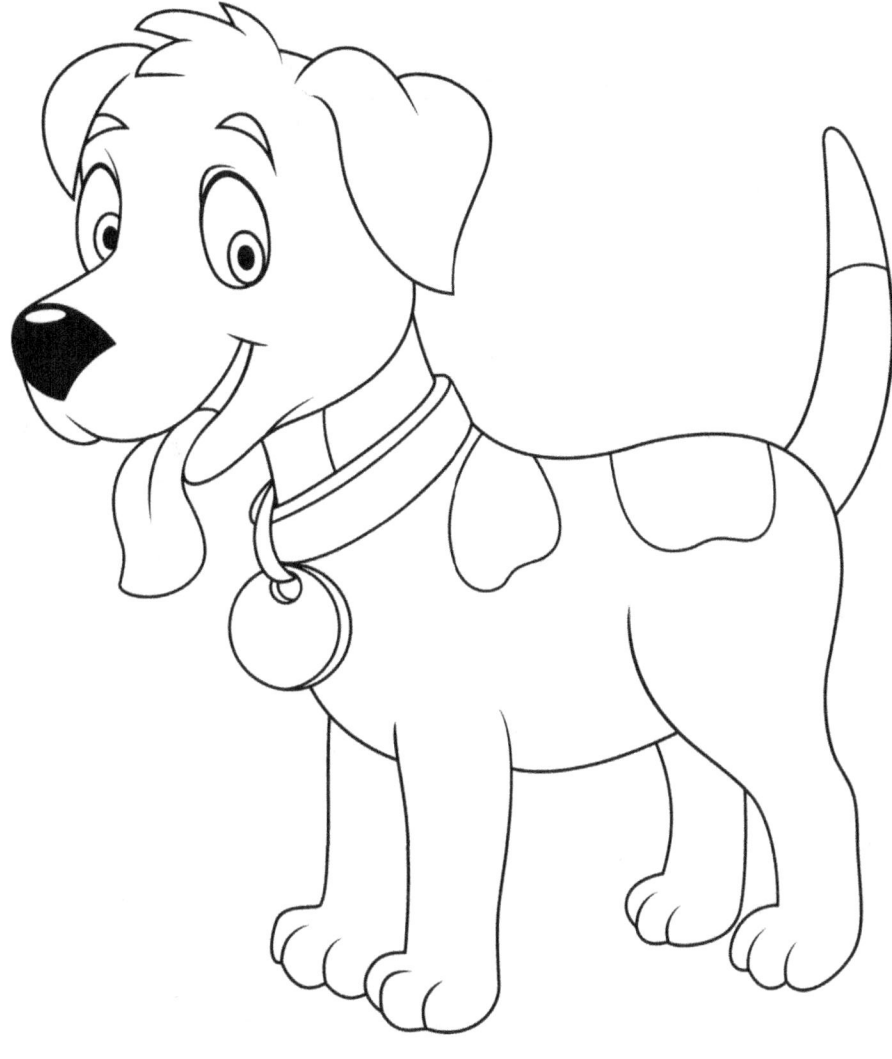

Dog

Dog
_____
_____
_____

Donut

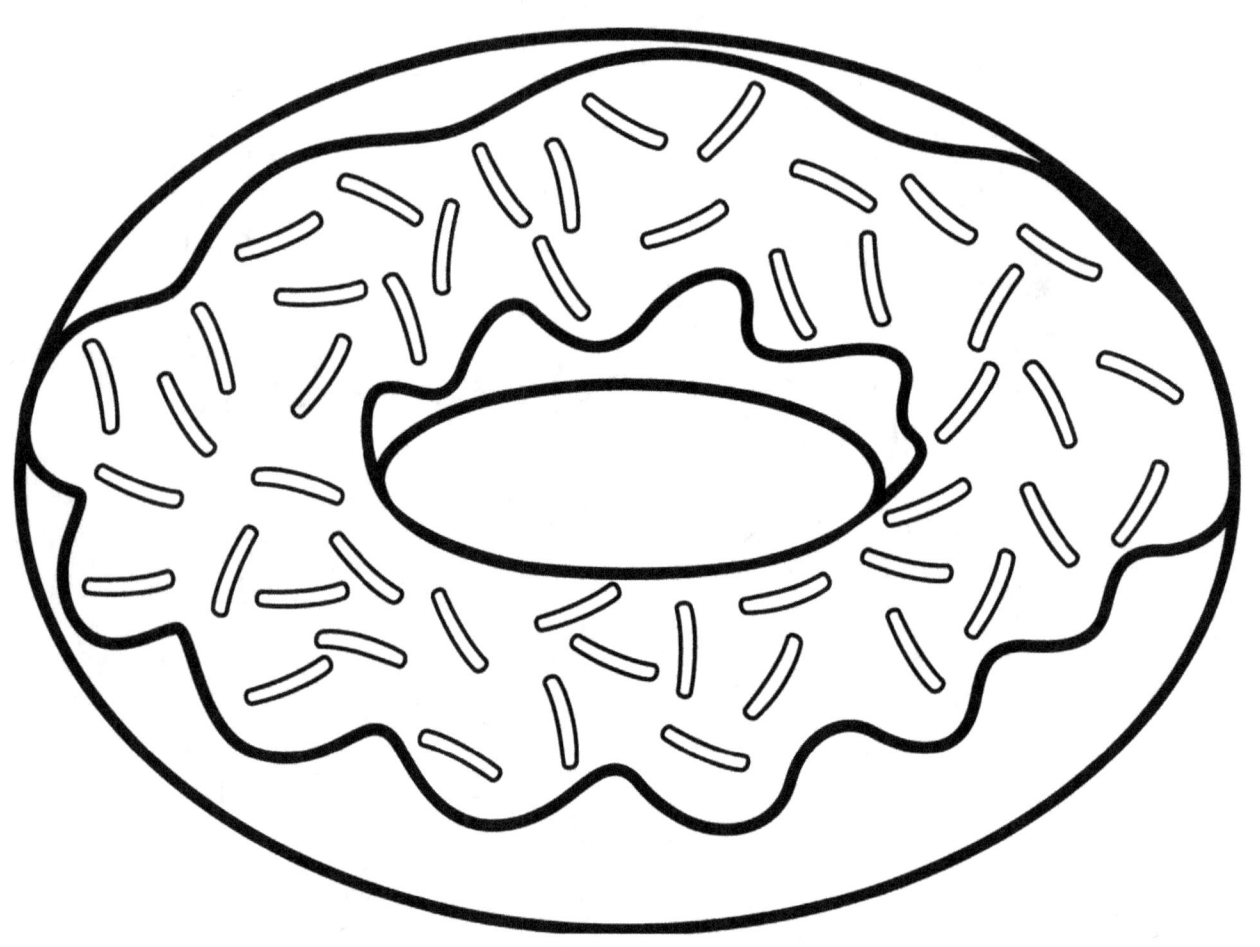

Donut

Donut
_____

_____

_____

Trommel

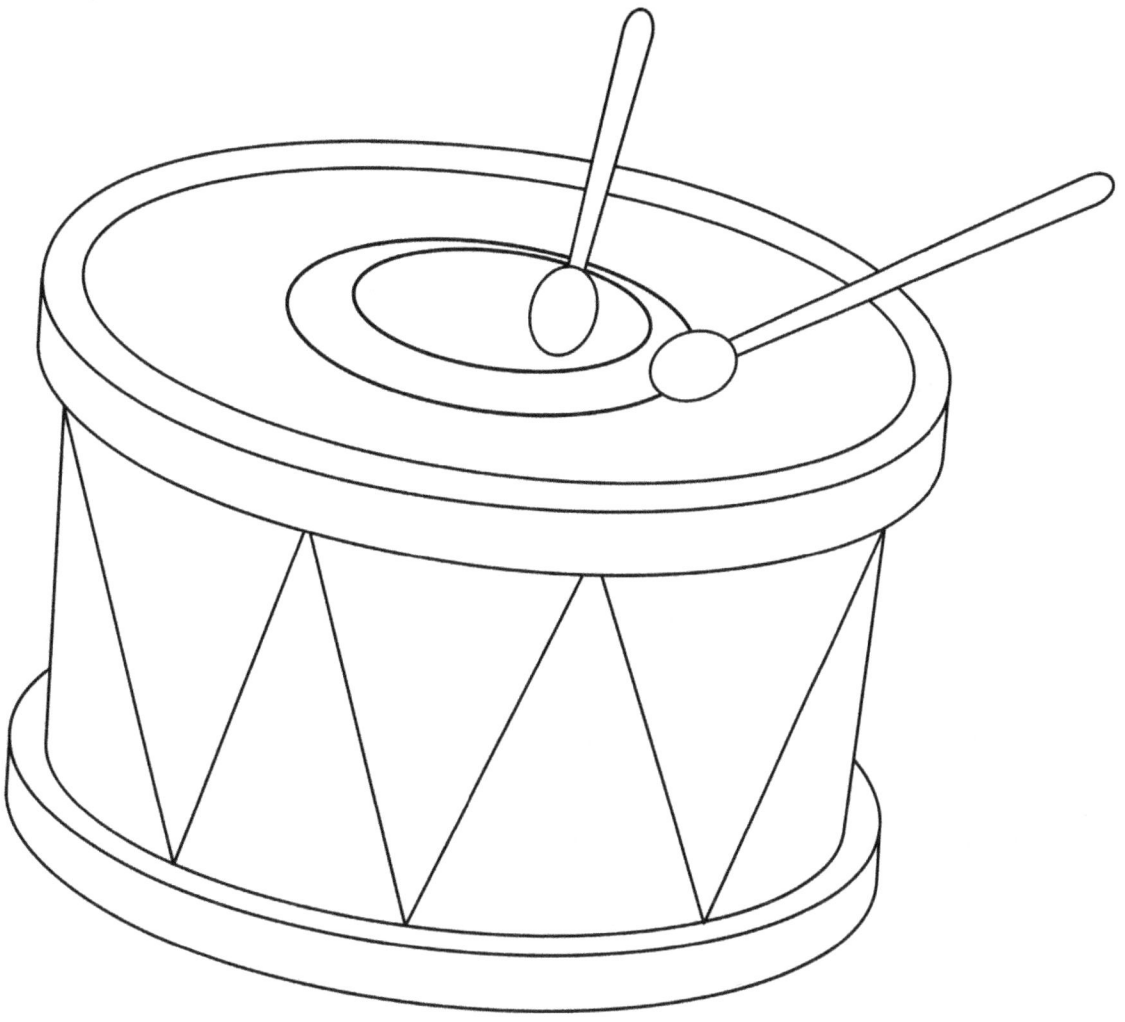

Drum

Drum

Mais

_o_n

Hund

_o_

Donut

Do_ut

Trommel

_ru_

Schnecke

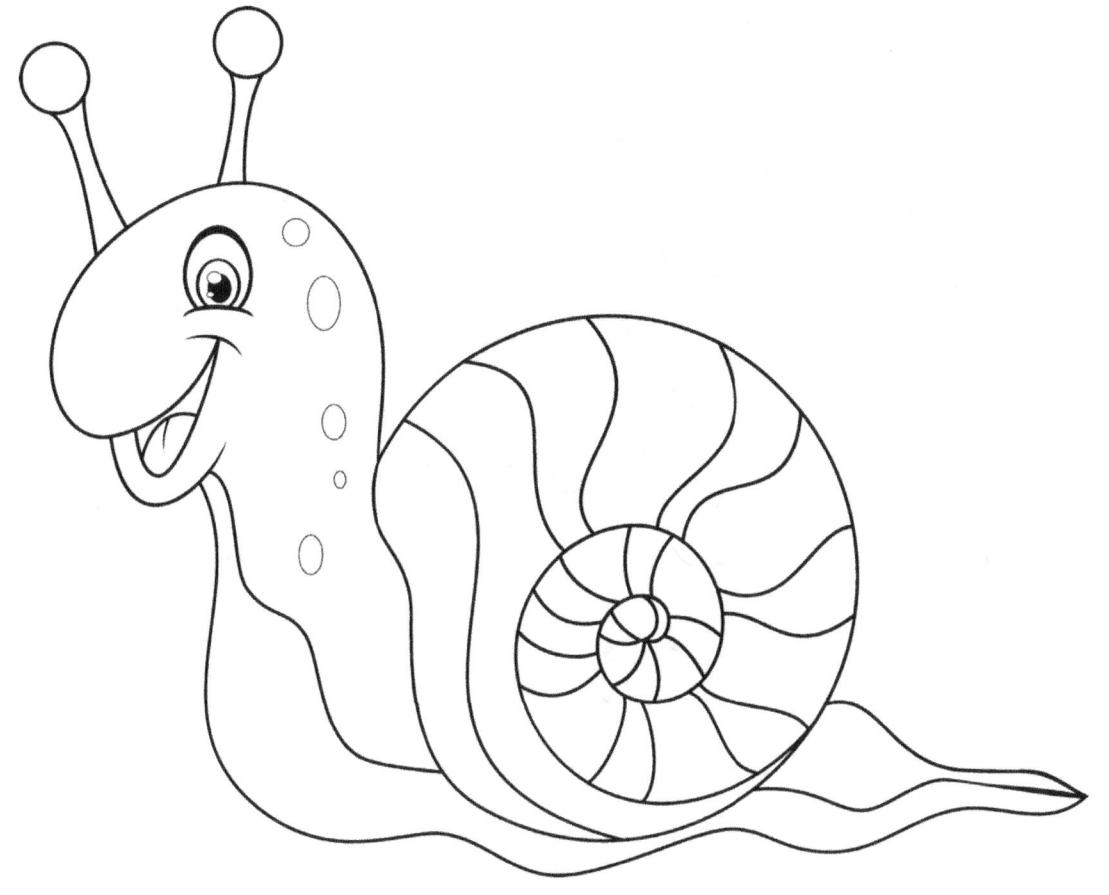

Snail

Snail

Zebra

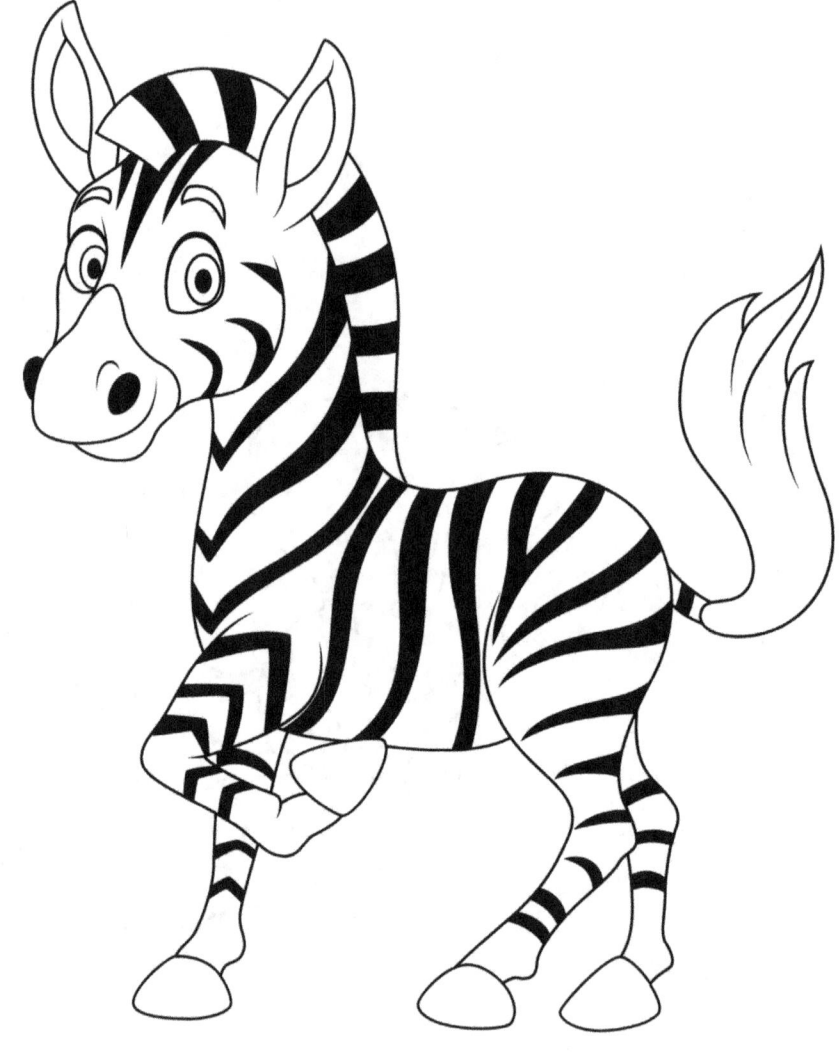

Zebra

Zebra
_____

_____

_____

Elefant

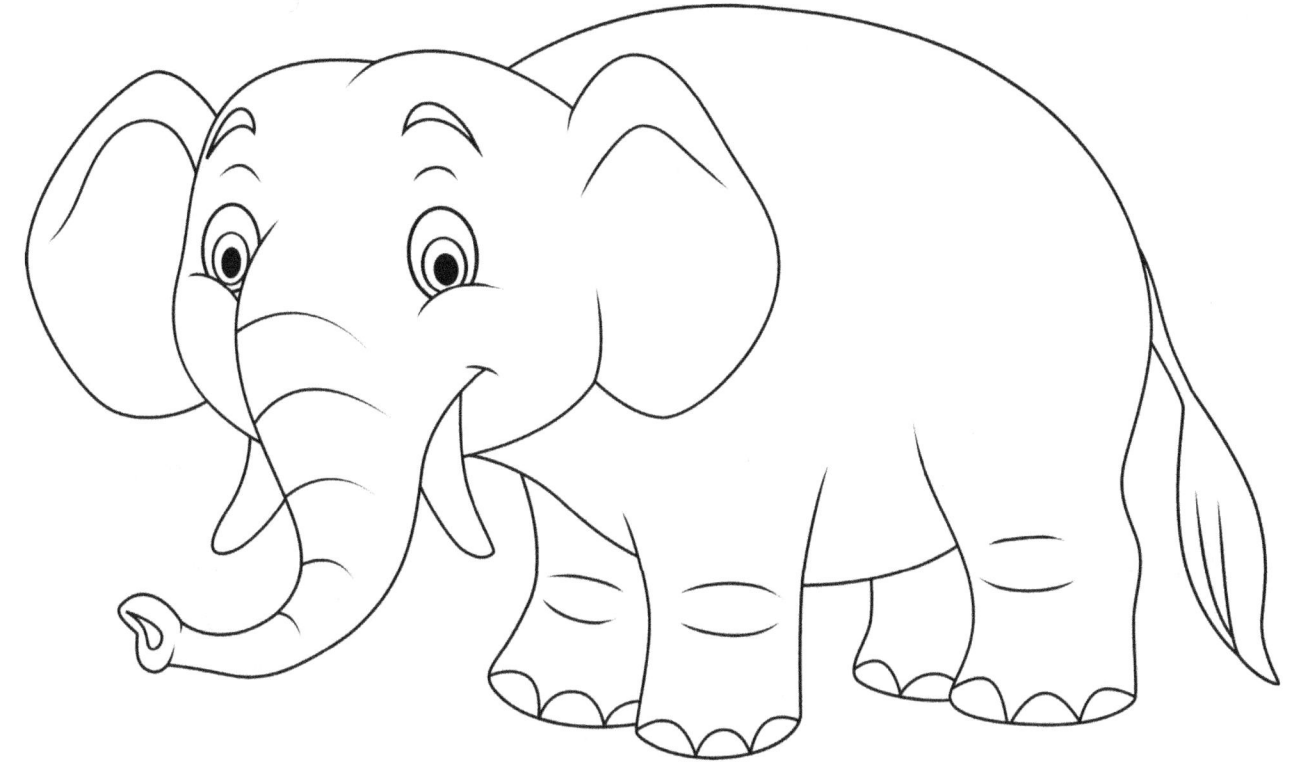

Elephant

Elephant

Fisch

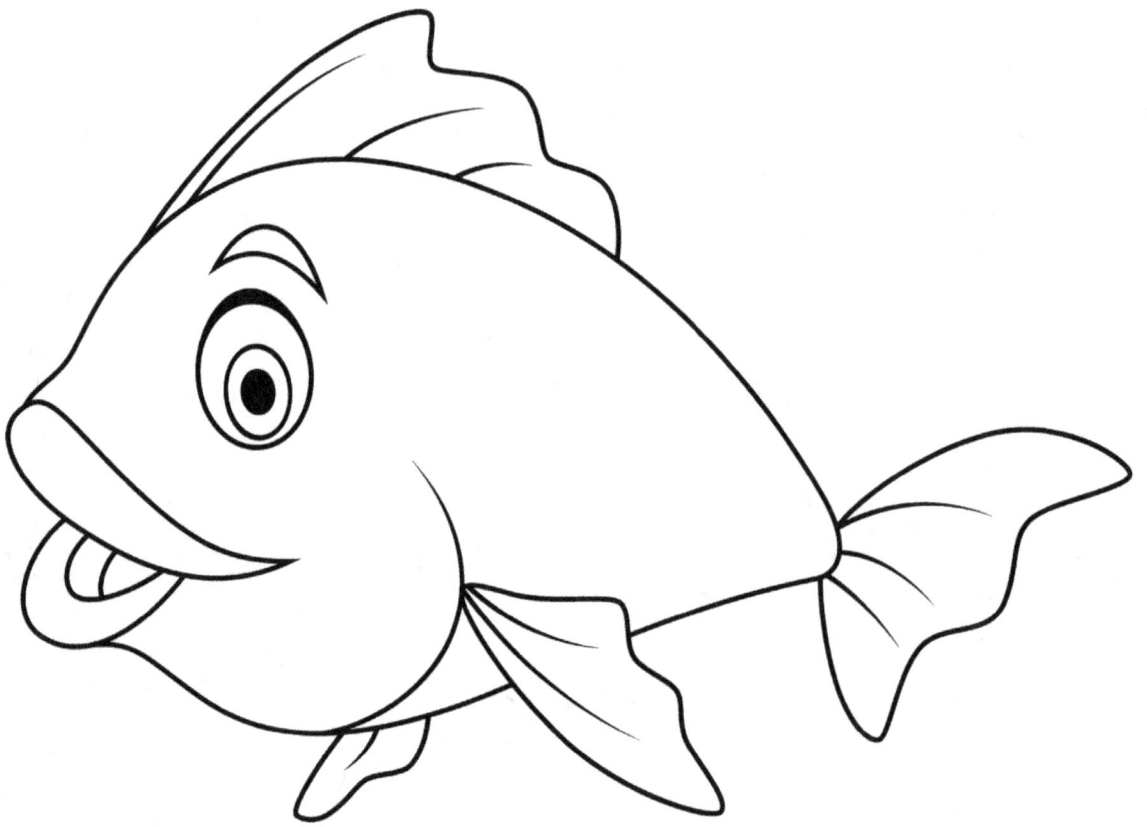

Fish

Fish
_____
_____
_____

Schnecke

S__il

Zebra

Ze_ra

Elefant

__ephant

Fisch

_is_

Blume

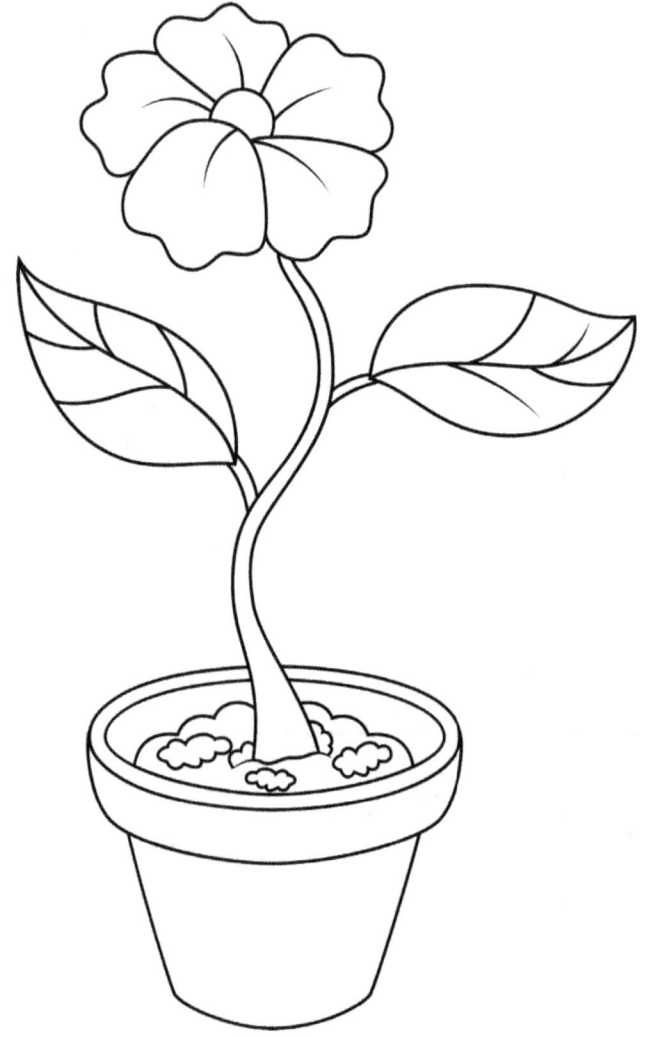

Flower

Flower
_____

_____

_____

Fuchs

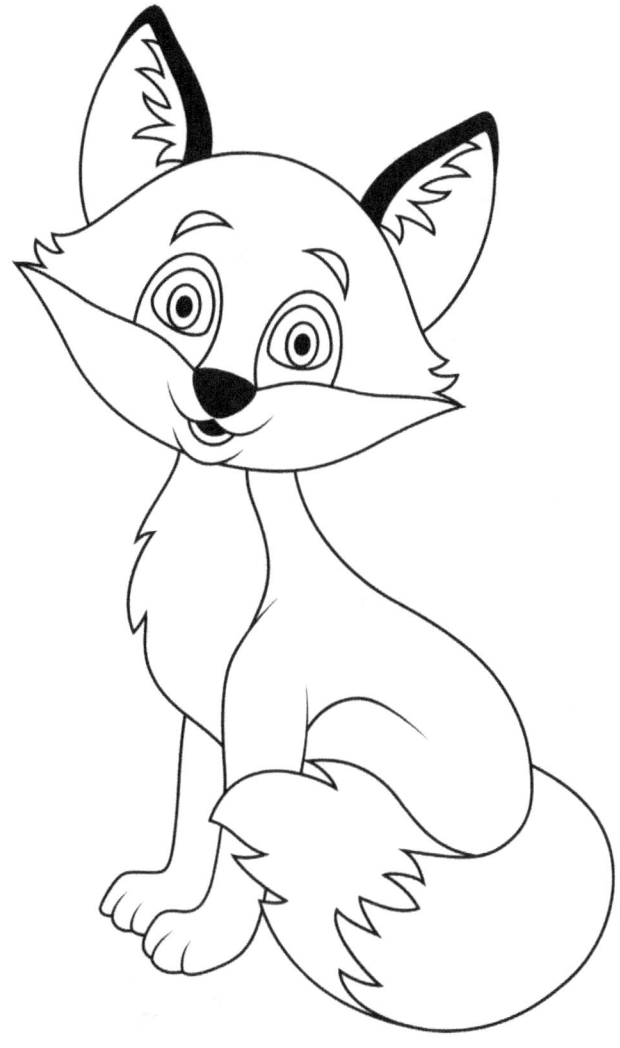

Fox

Fox
_____
_____
_____

Giraffe

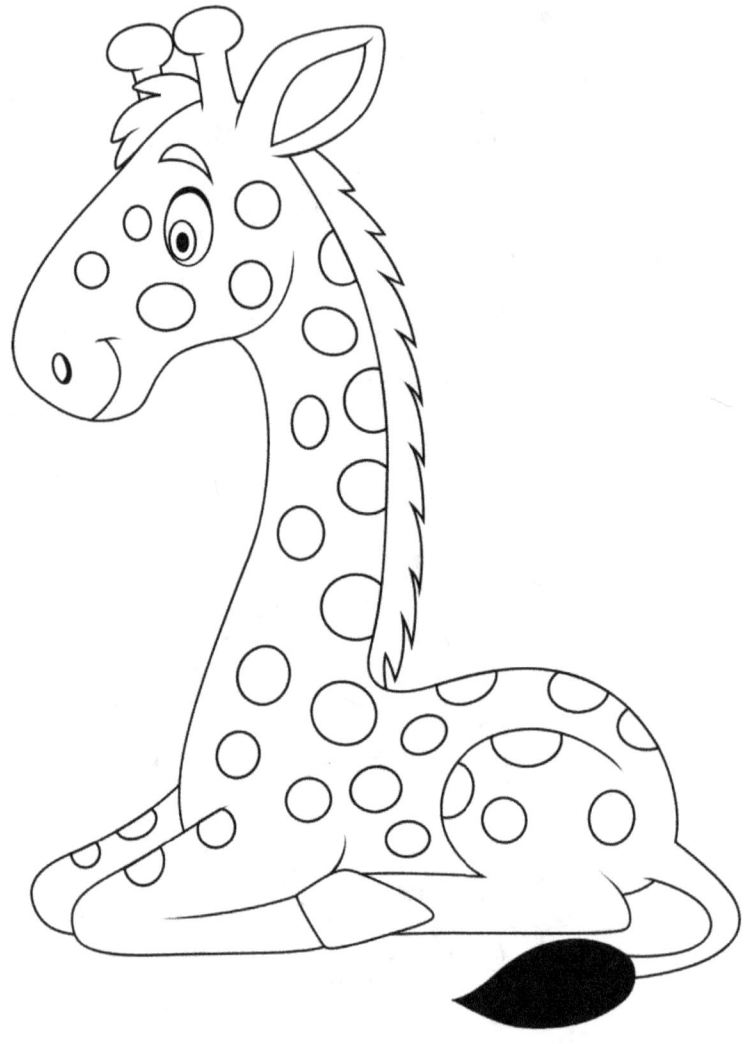

Giraffe

Giraffe
_____

_____

_____

Brille

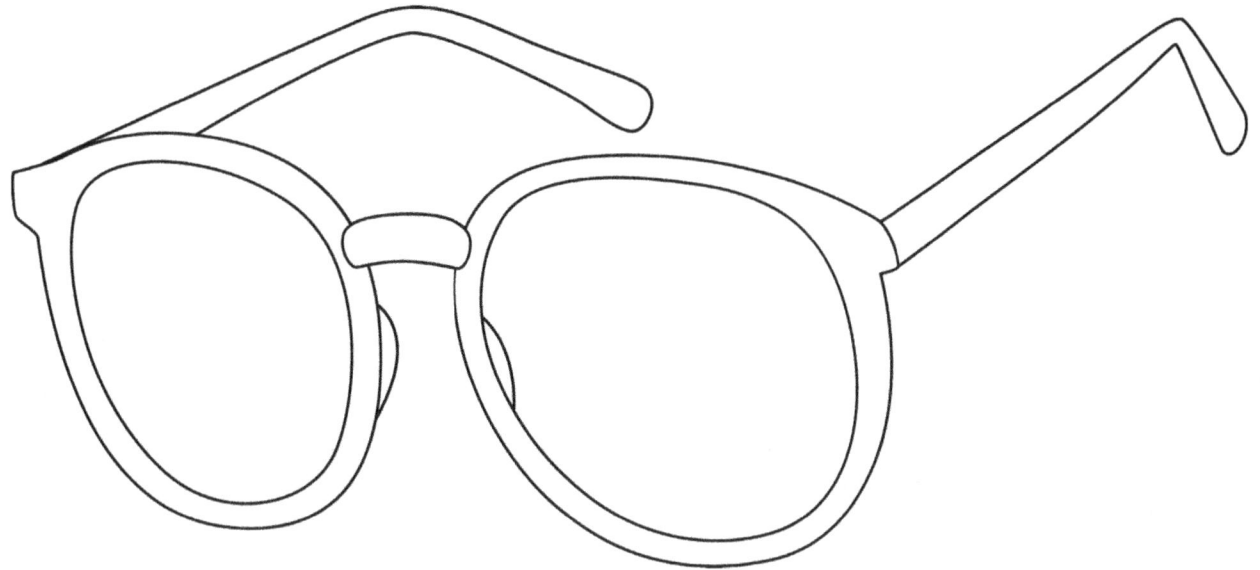

Glasses

Glasses

Blume

F__wer

Fuchs

_o_

Giraffe

iraff

Brille

G_a_ses

Weintrauben

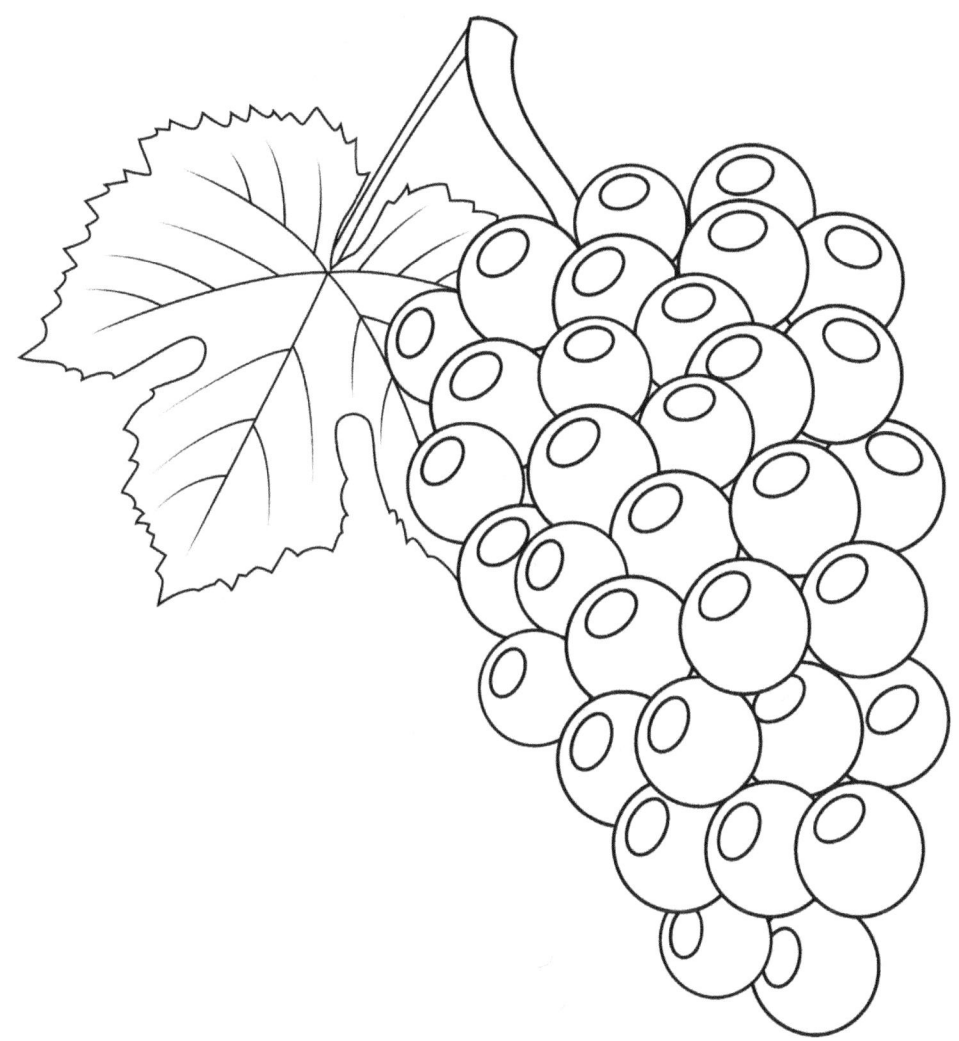

Grapes

Grapes

Hamburger

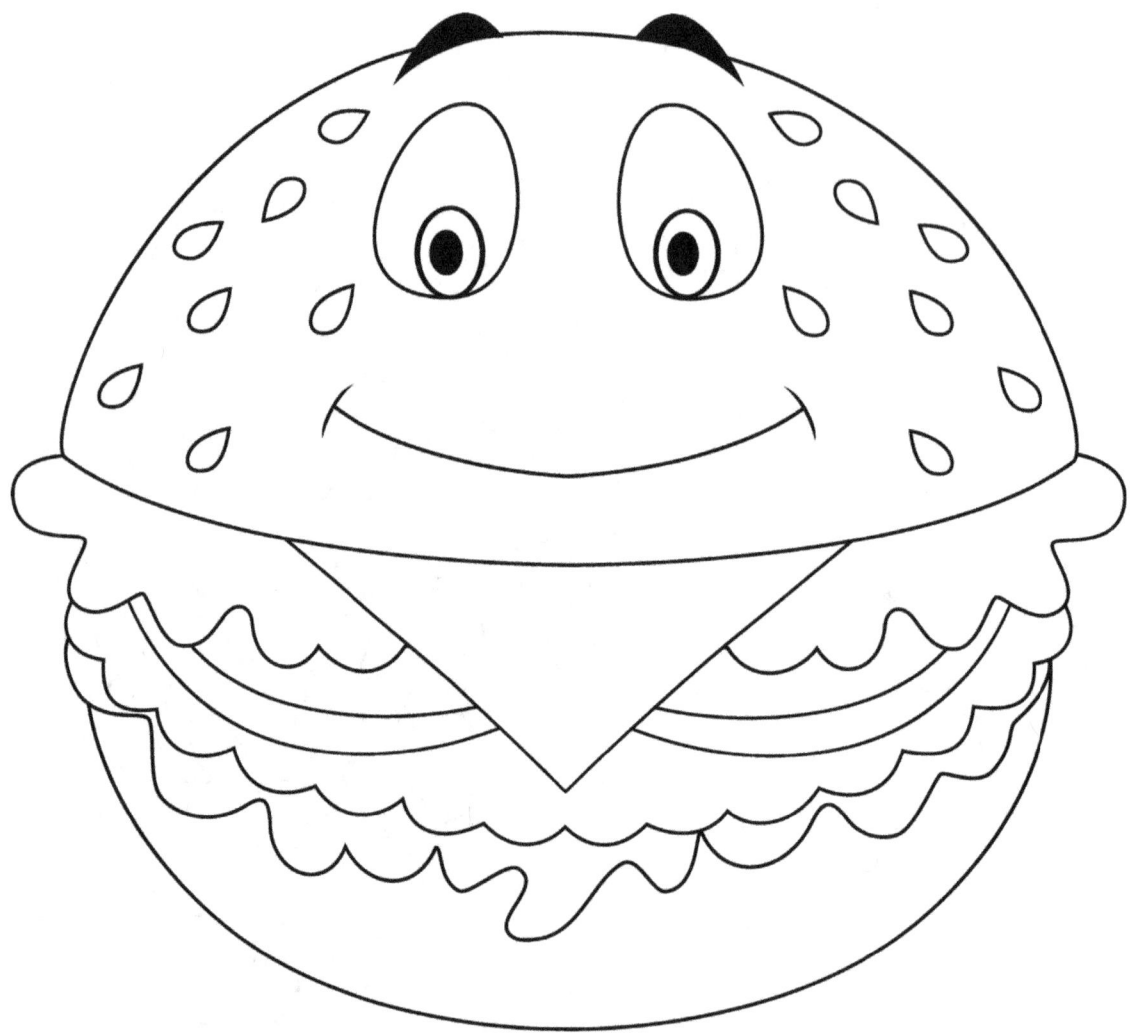

Hamburger

Hamburger

Flusspferd

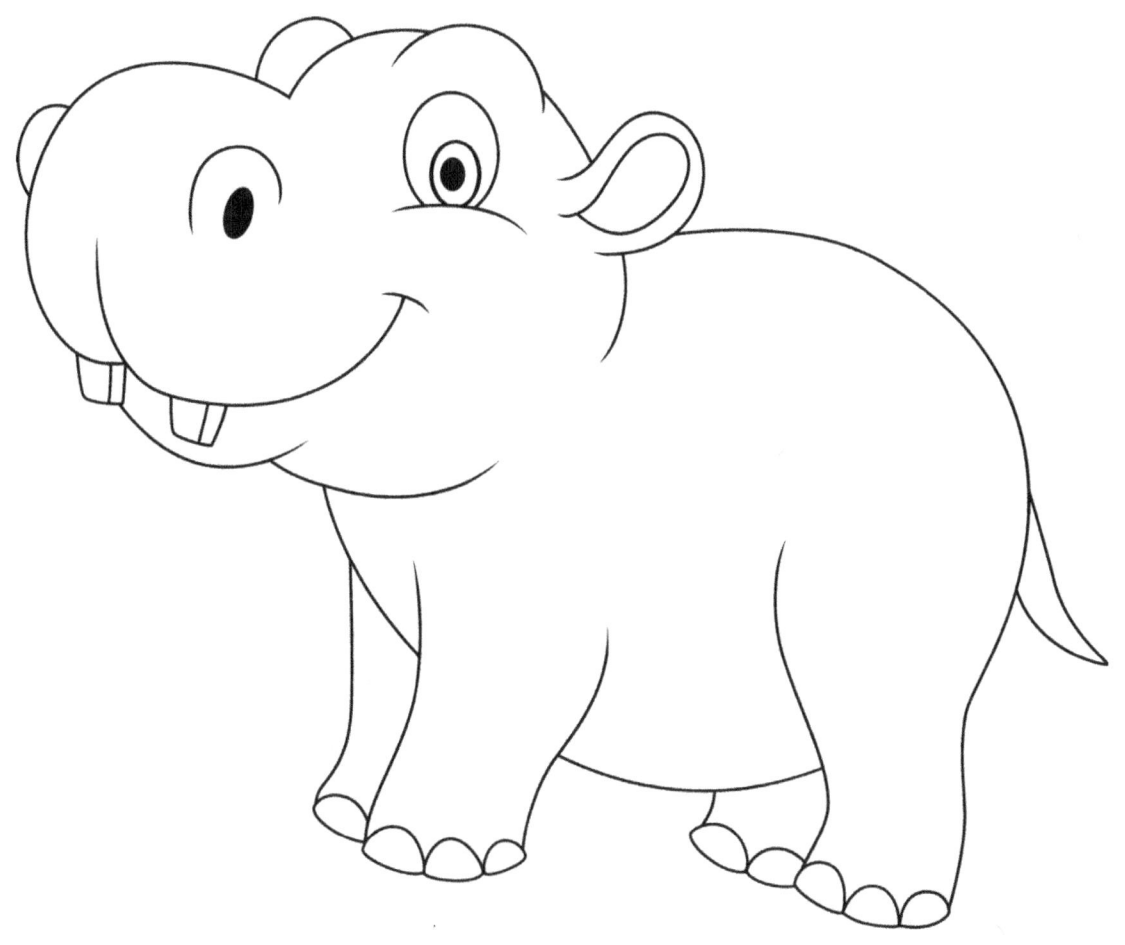

Hippo

Hippo

Haus

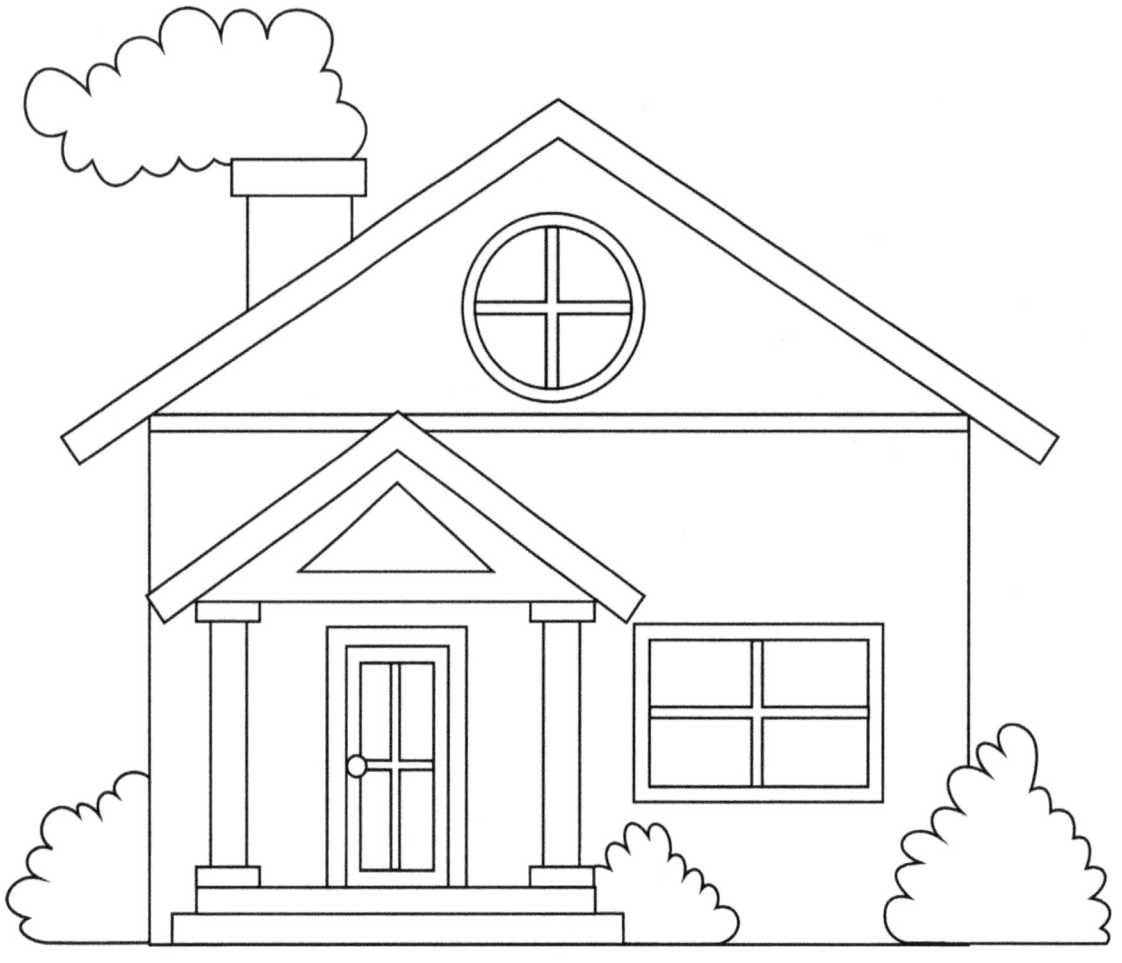

House

House
_____

_____

_____

Weintrauben

G_ape_

Hamburger

Ha_b_rger

Flusspferd

H_pp_

Haus

H_us_

Eiscreme

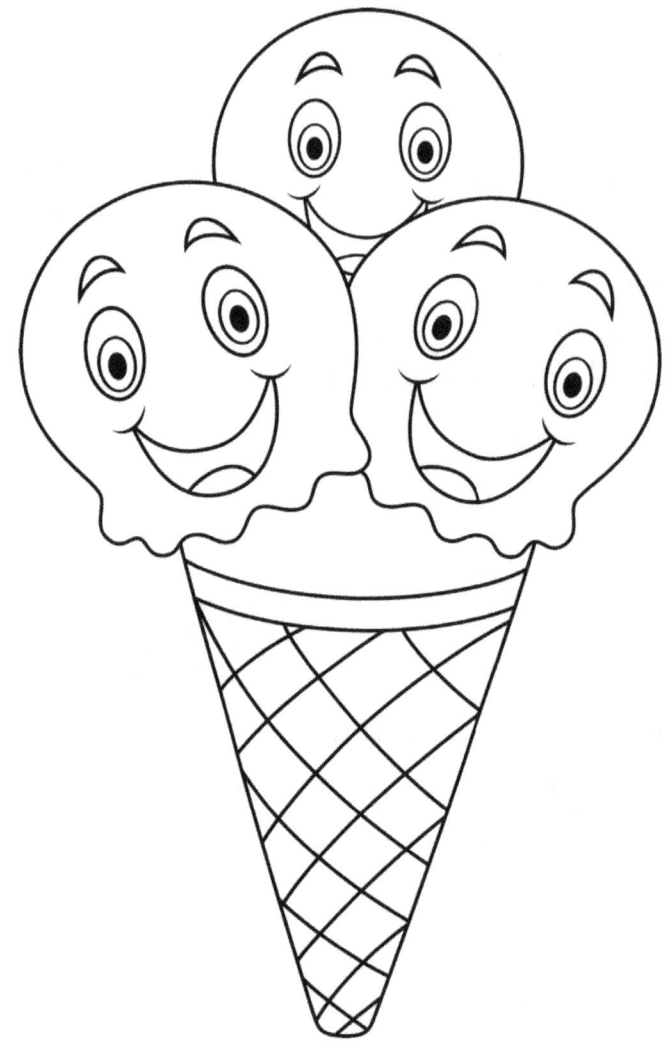

Ice cream

Ice cream
_____

_____

_____

Leguan

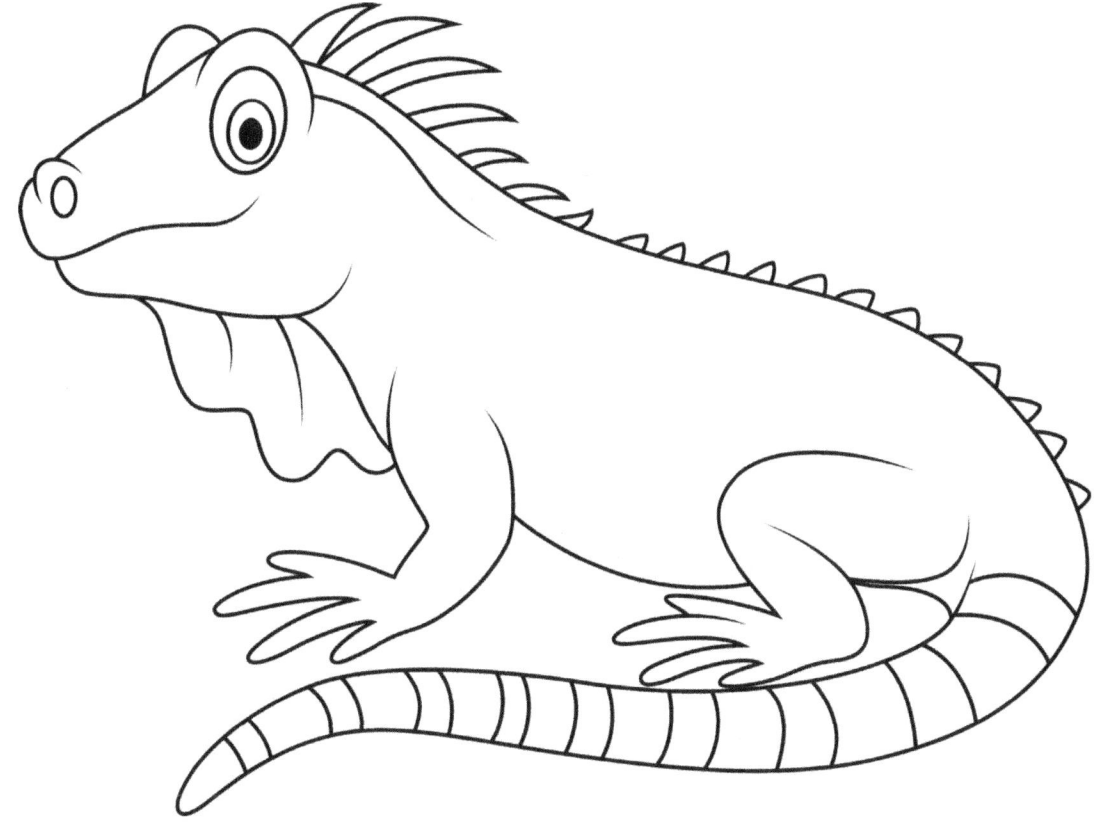

Iguana

Iguana

Ente

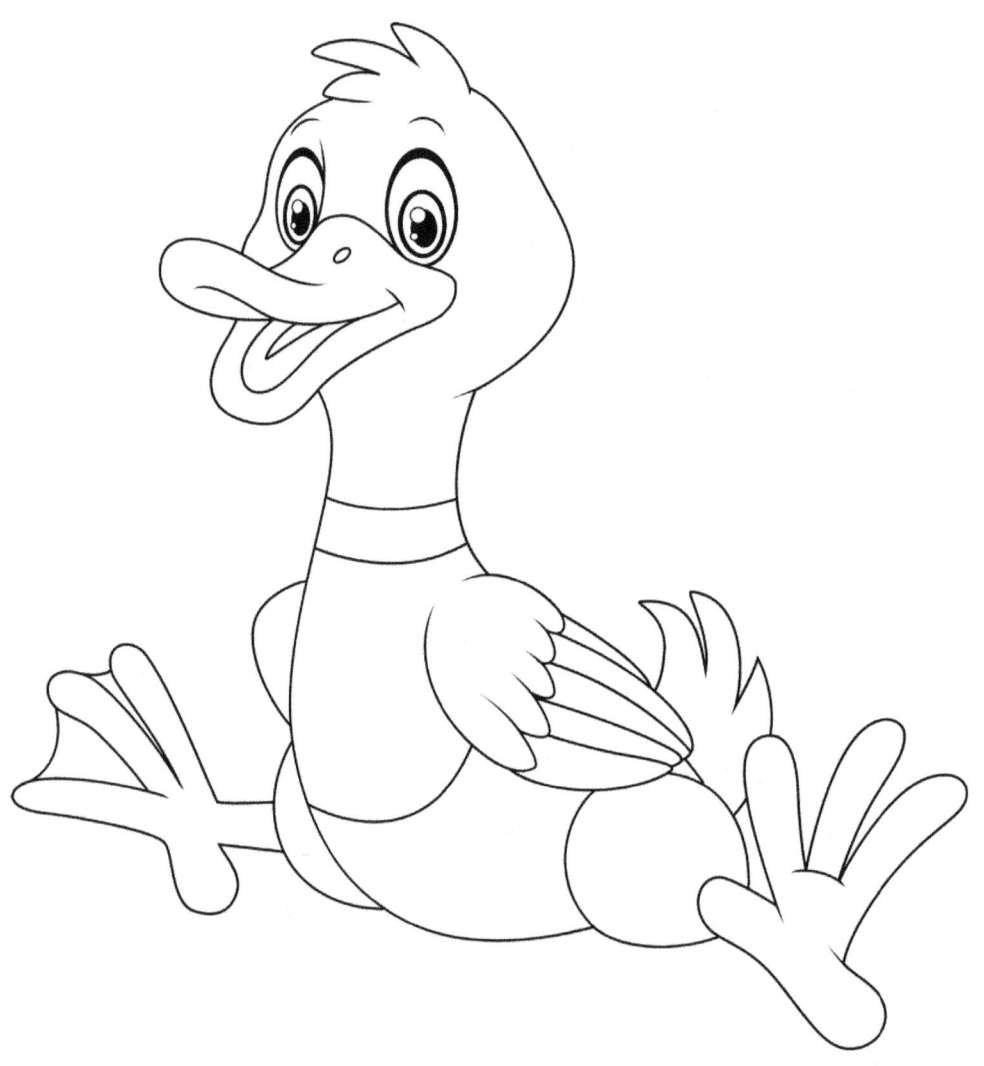

Duck

Duck

Jaguar

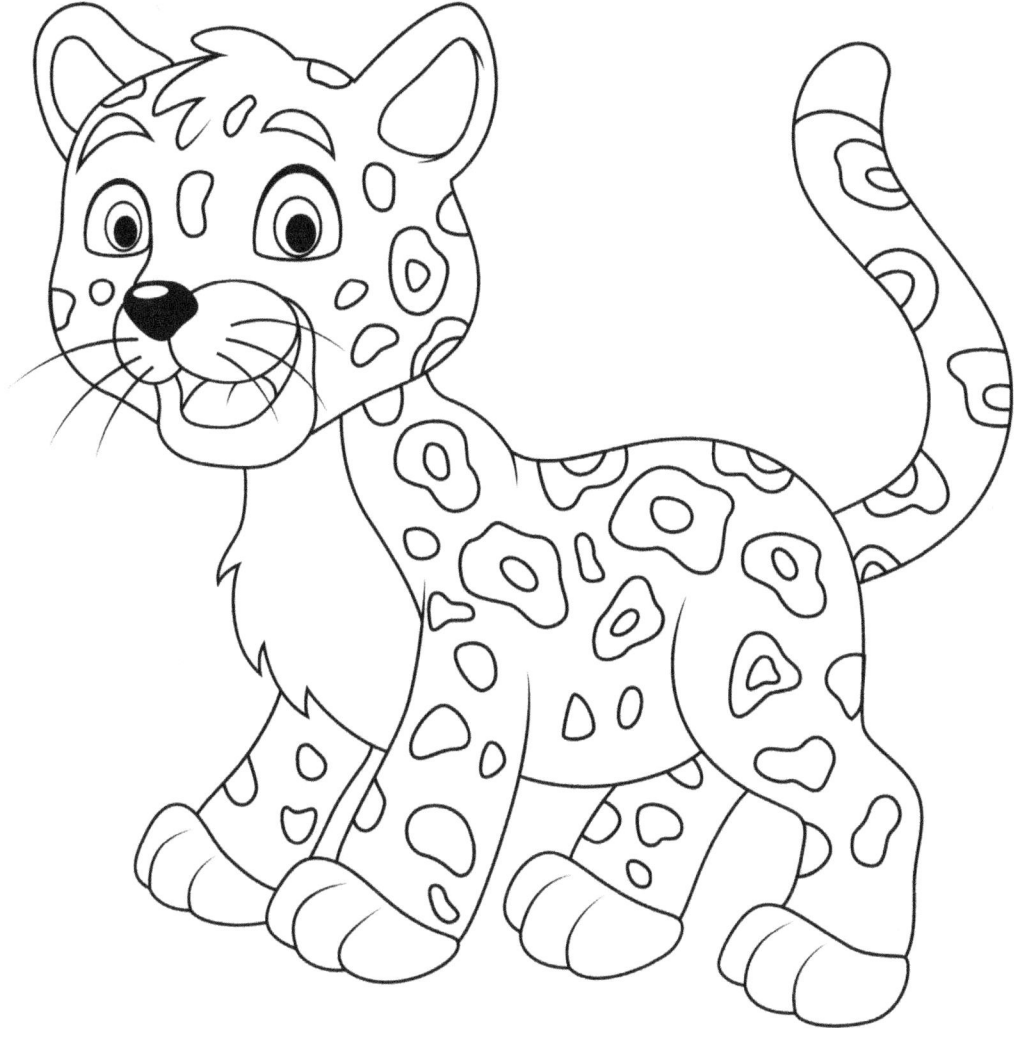

Jaguar

Jaguar

Eiscreme

ce crea

Leguan

Ig__na

Ente

D__k

Jaguar

Ja_ua_

Marmelade

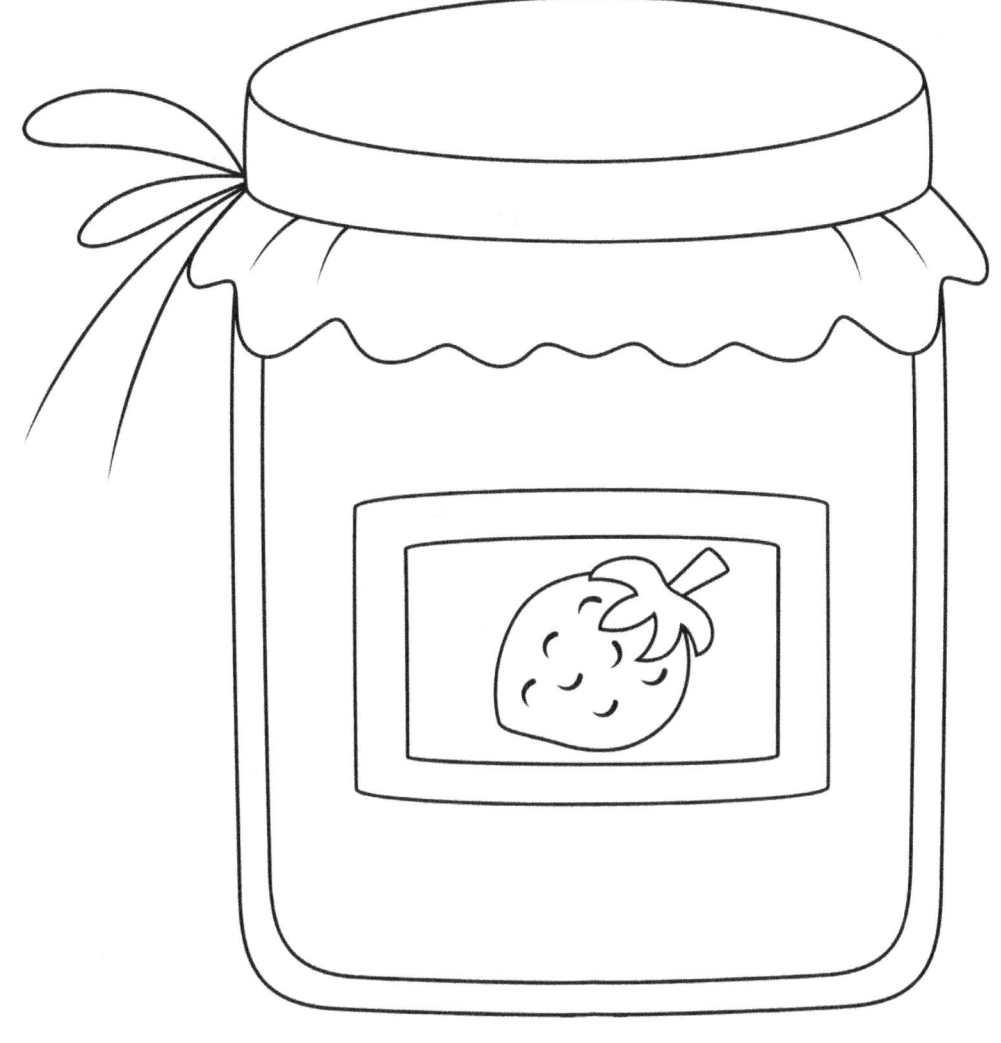

Jam

Jam

Qualle

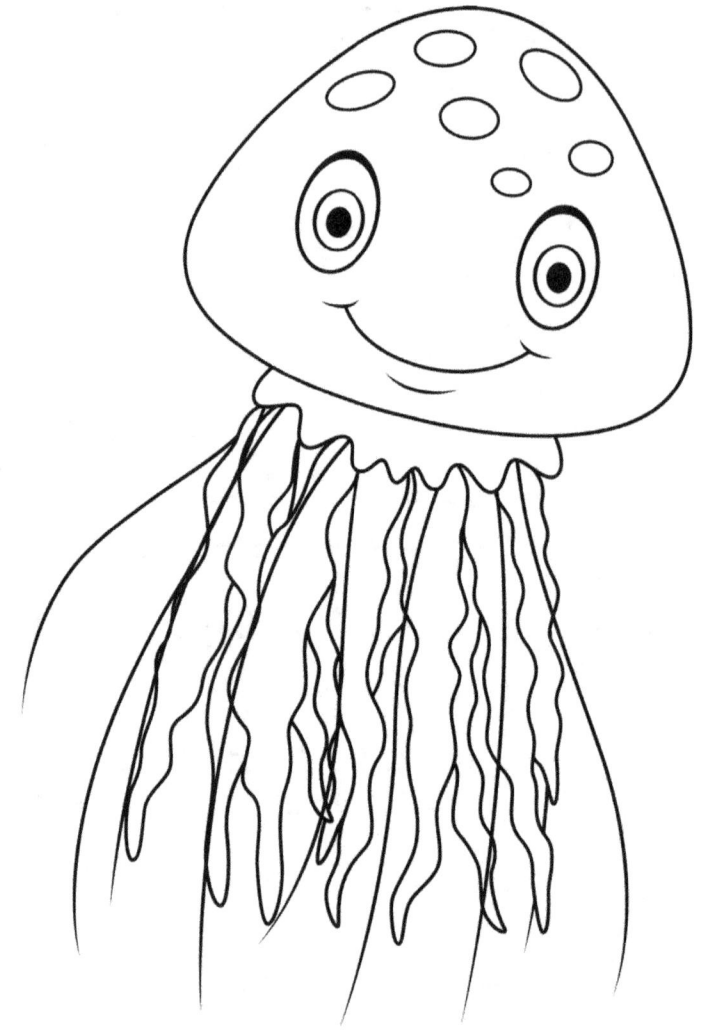

Jellyfish

Jellyfish
_____

_____

_____

Zeppelin

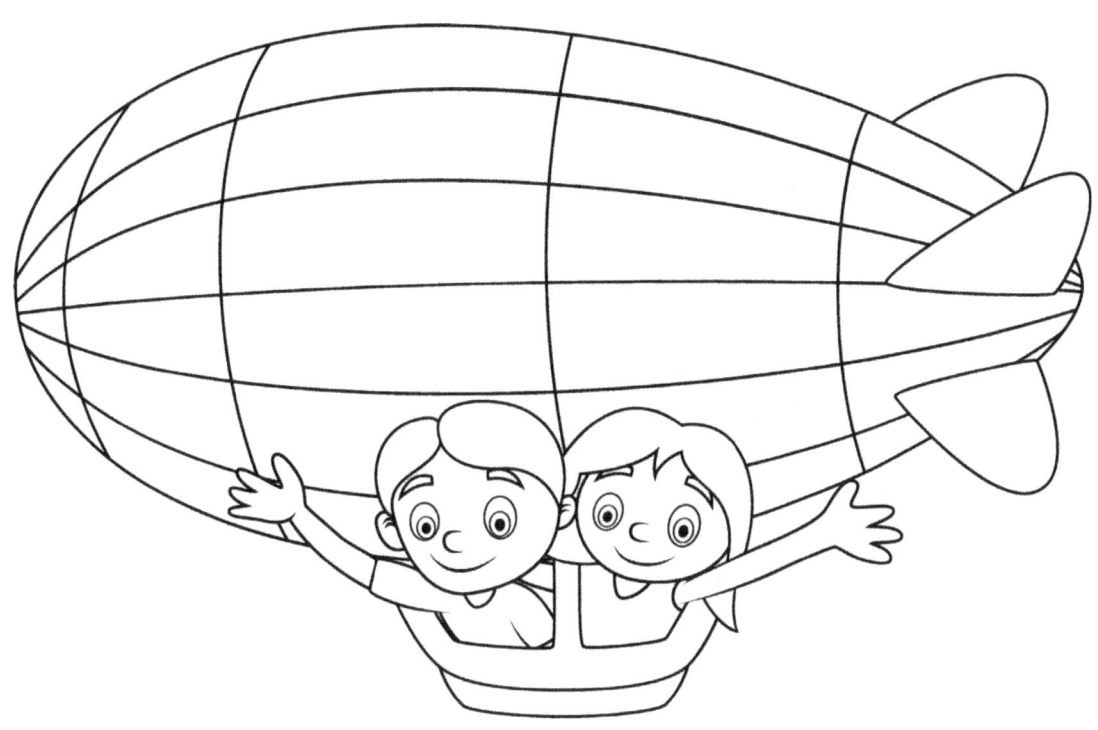

Zeppelin

Zeppelin

Kiwi

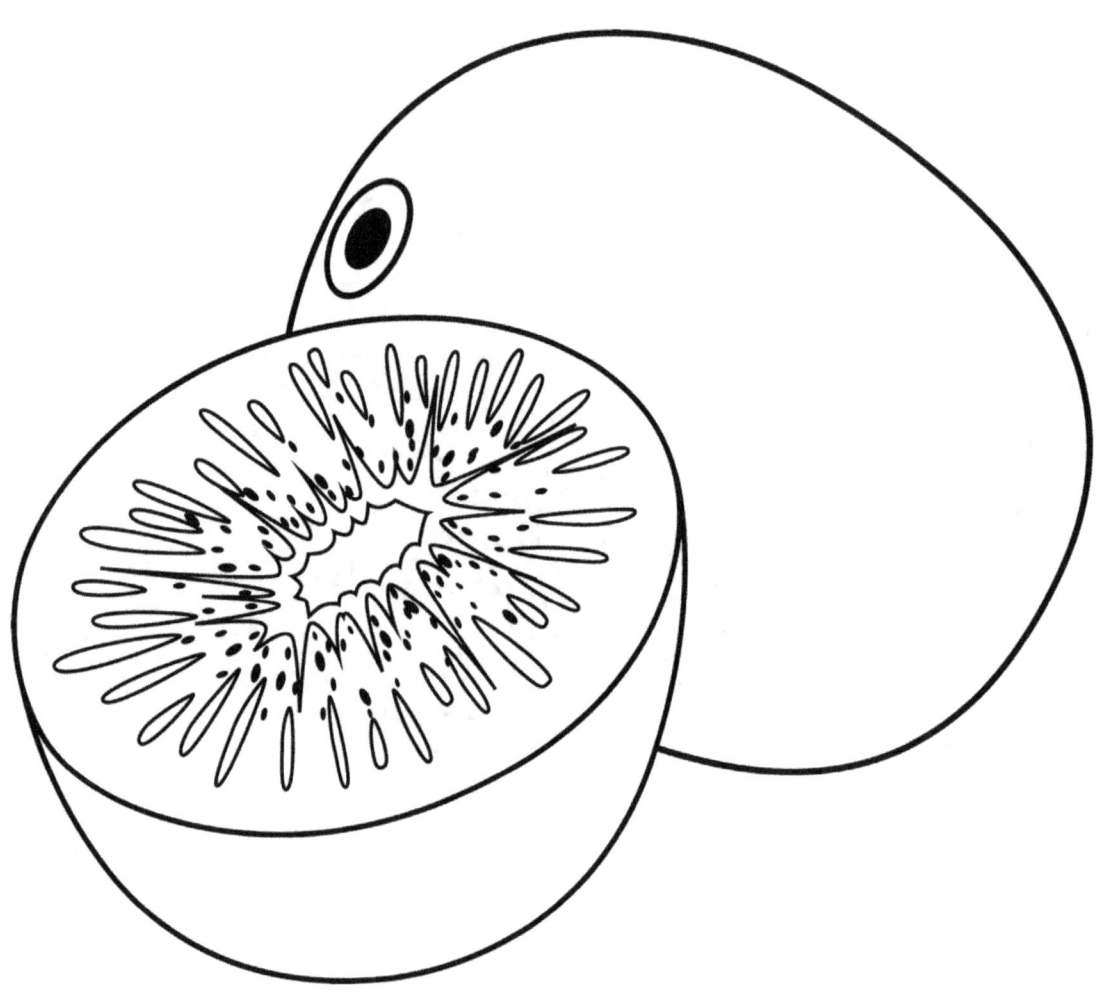

Kiwi

Kiwi

Marmelade

_am

Qualle

Je_lyfis_

Zeppelin

_e_pelin

Kiwi

K__i

Erdbeere

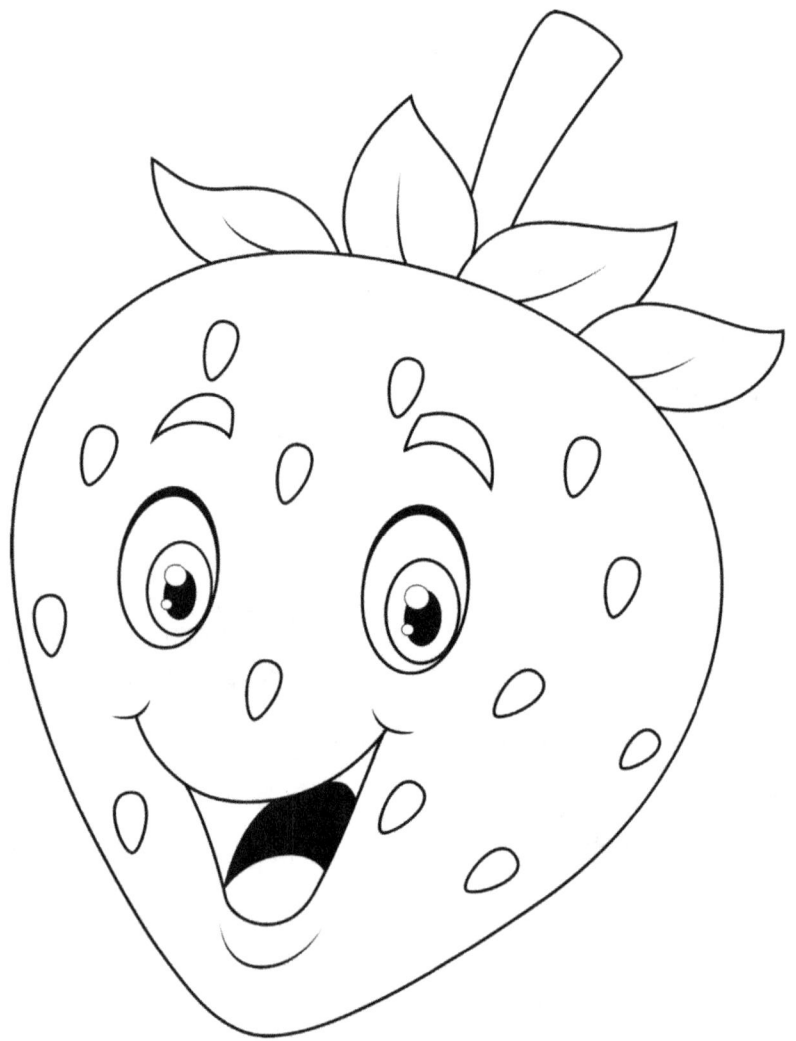

Strawberry

Strawberry

Blätter

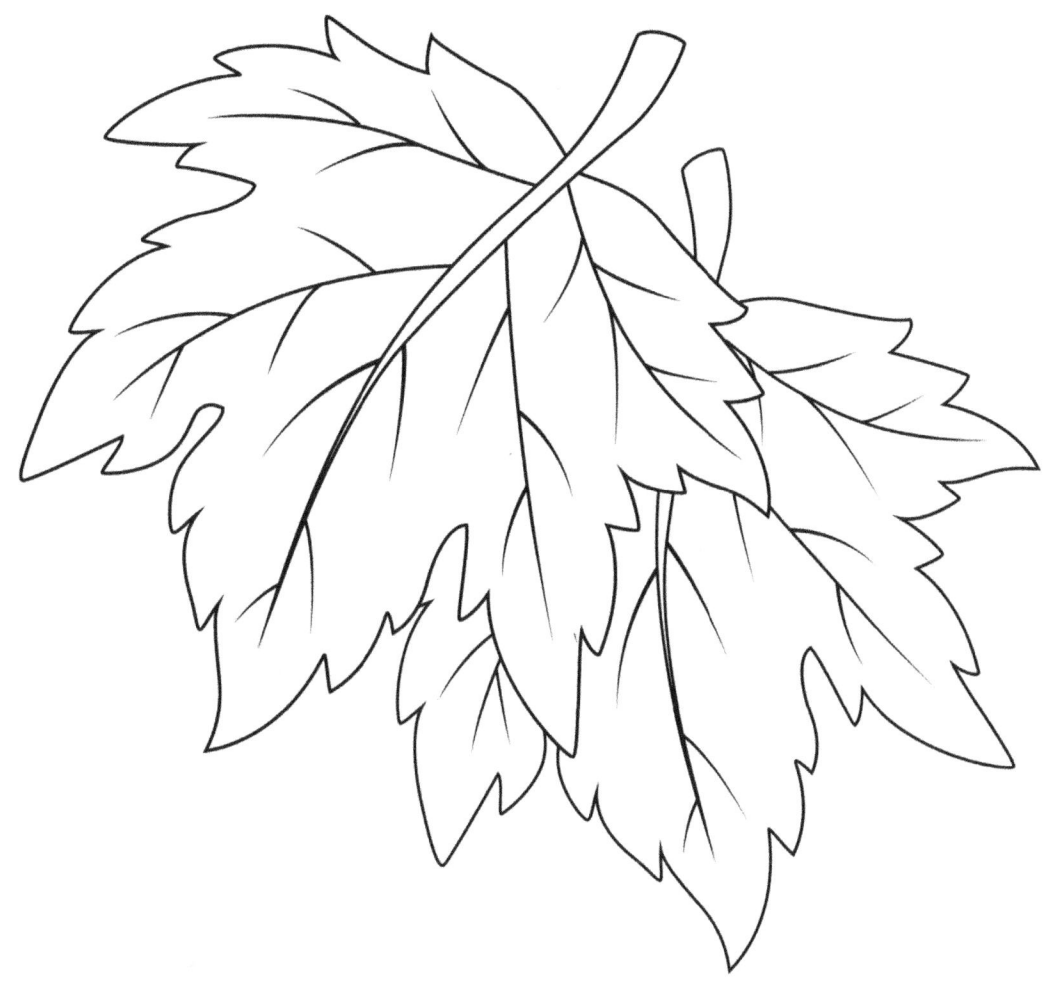

Leaves

Leaves

Lampe

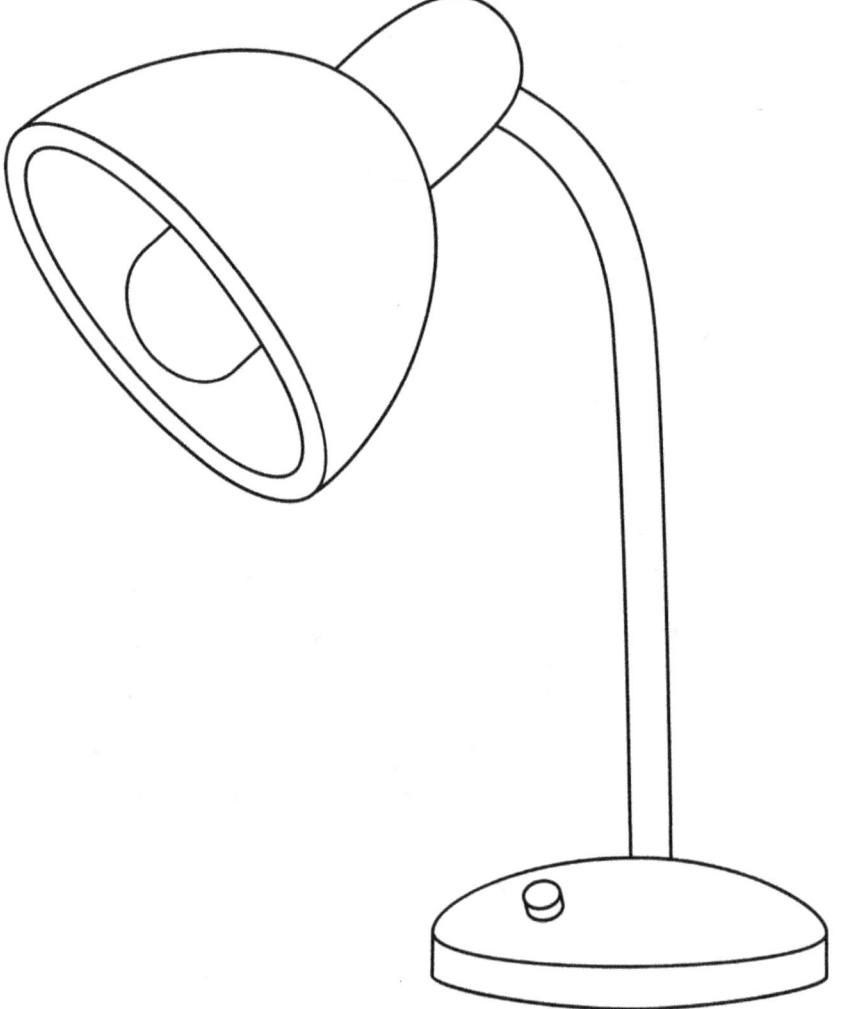

Lights

Lights

Löwe

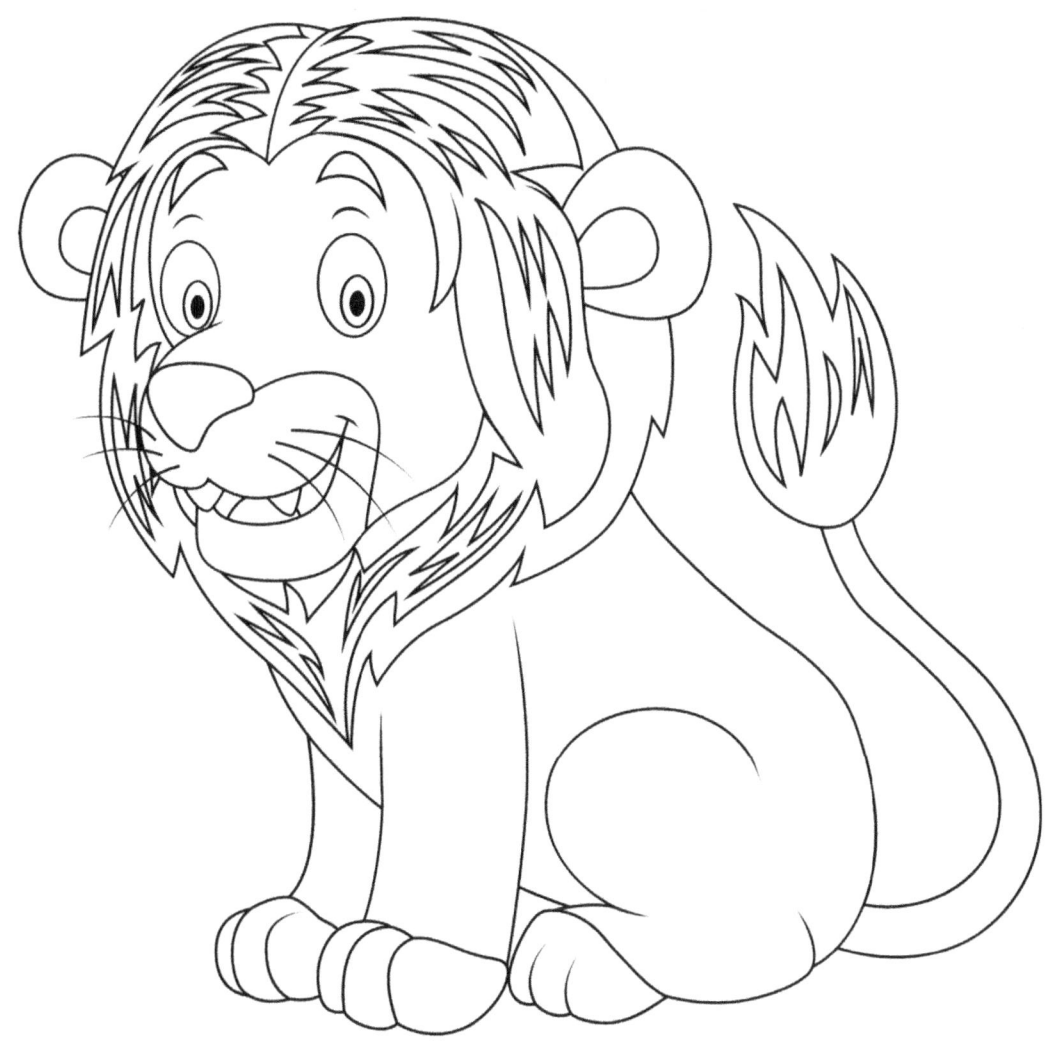

Lion

Lion
_____

_____

_____

Erdbeere	
	Strawber_y

Blätter	
	Lea_e_

Lampe	
	L_ght_

Löwe	
	_io_

Affe

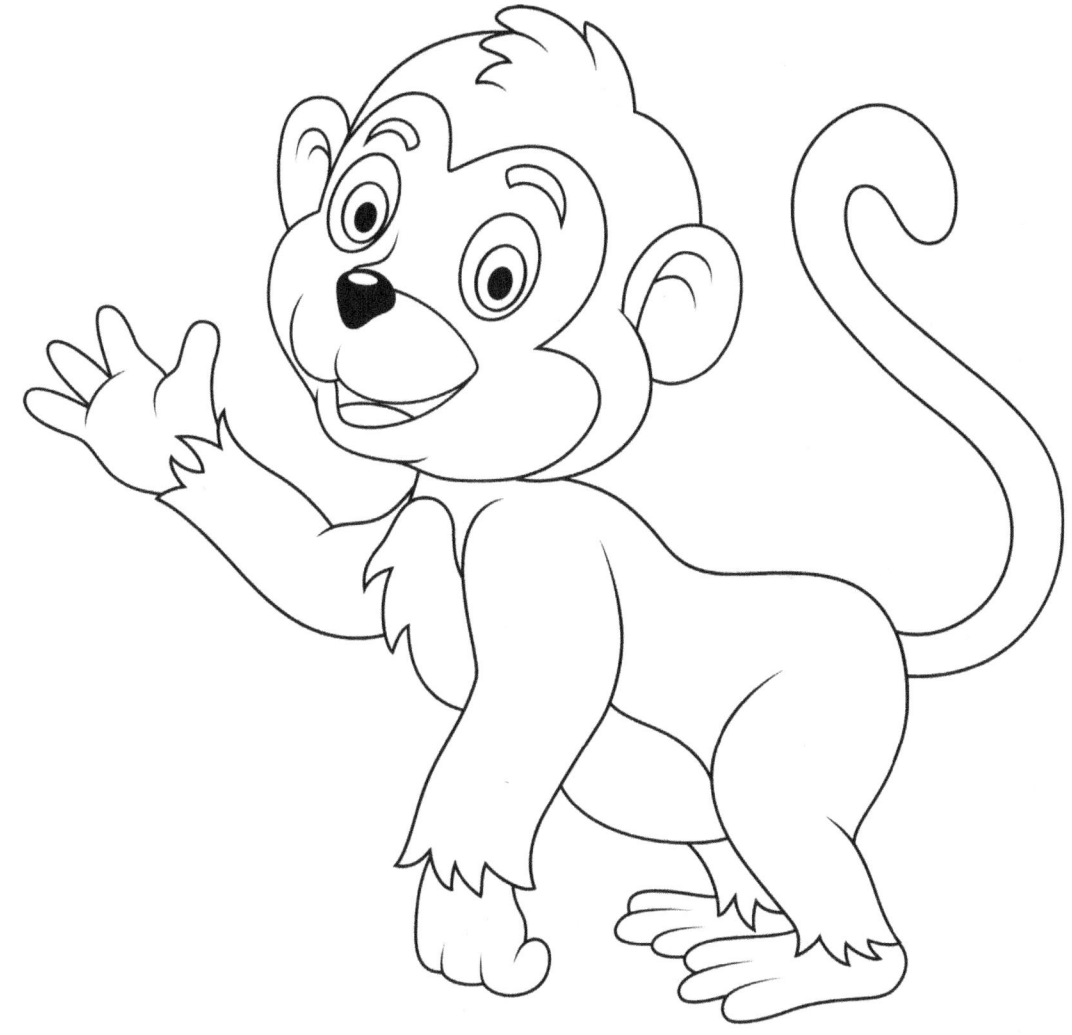

Monkey

Monkey

Maus

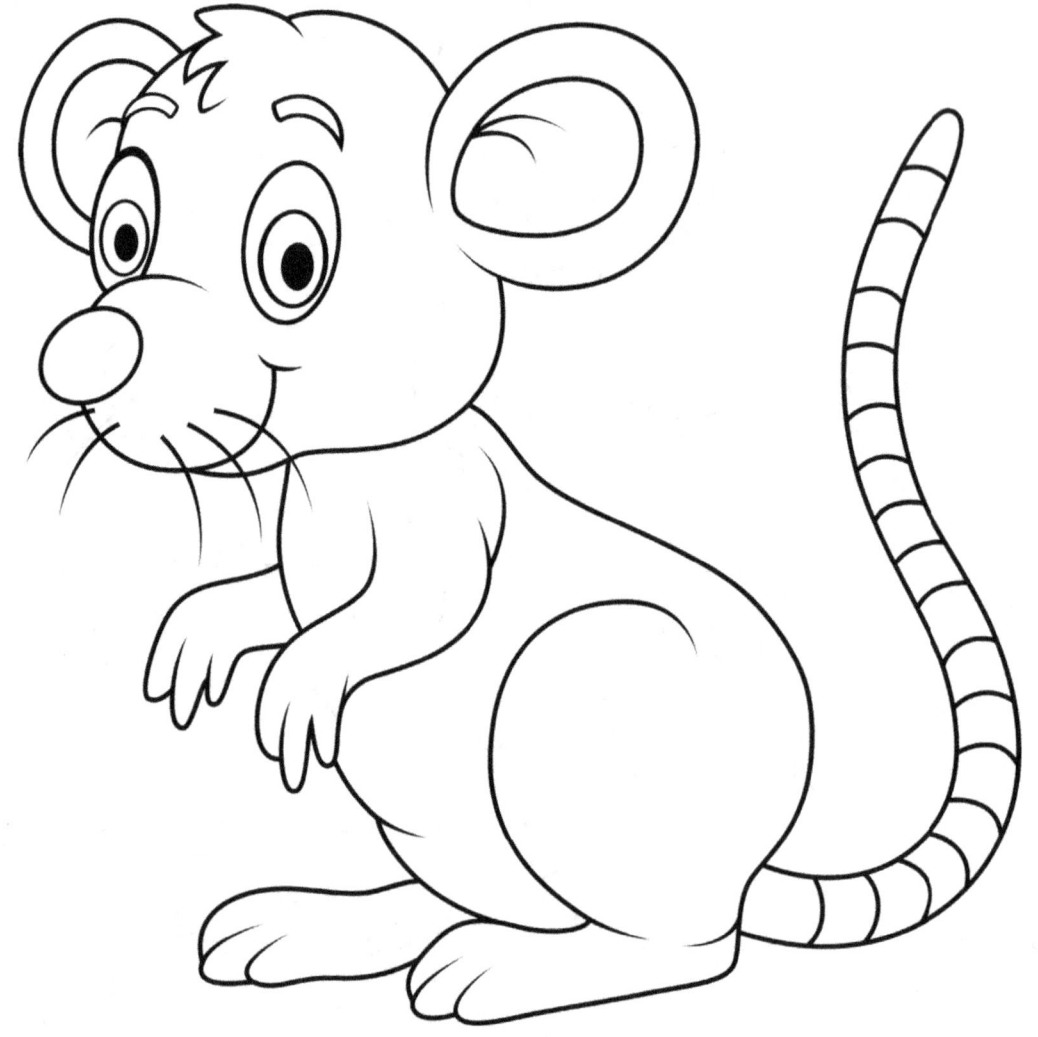

Mouse

Mouse
_____

_____

_____

Fliegenpilz

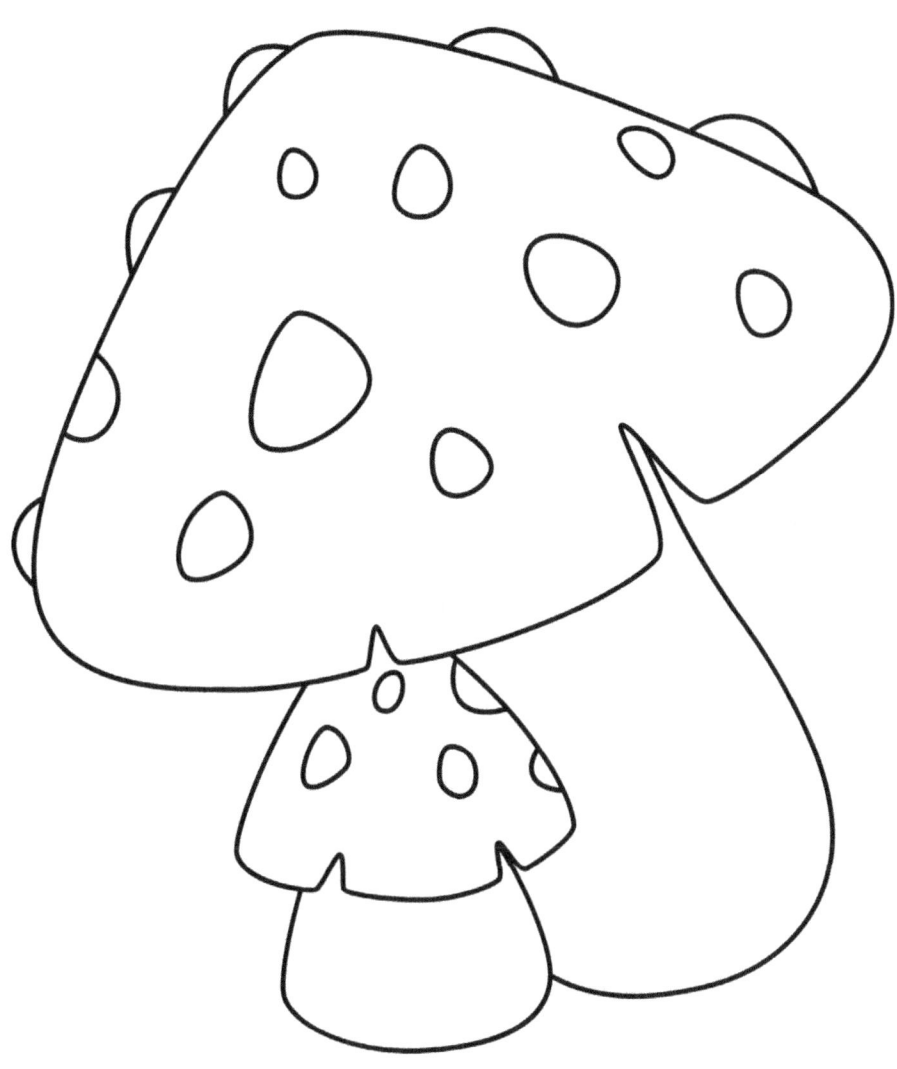

Fly agaric mushroom

Fly agaric mushroom

Nagel

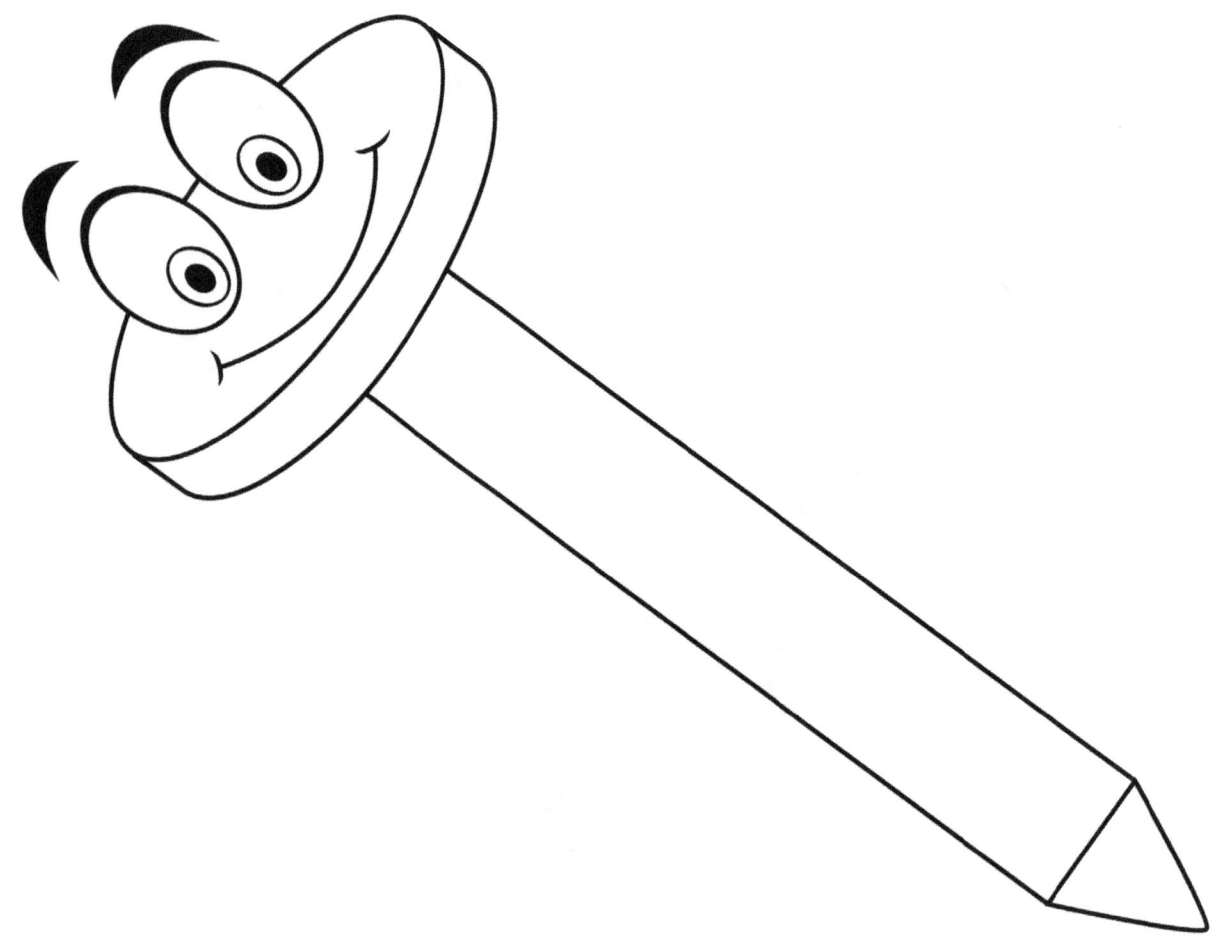

Nail

Nail

Affe

Mon_ey

Maus

M__se

Fliegenpilz

F_y agaric mu_hroom

Nagel

_ai_

Pferd

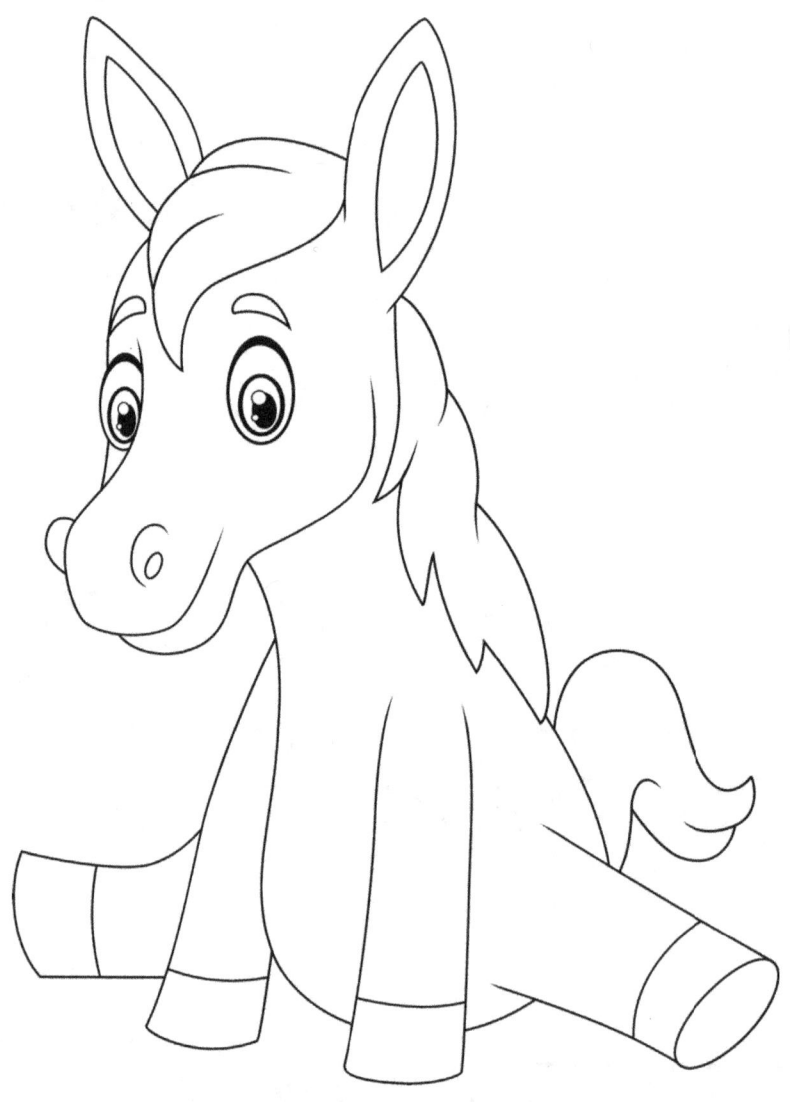

Horse

Horse

Nuss

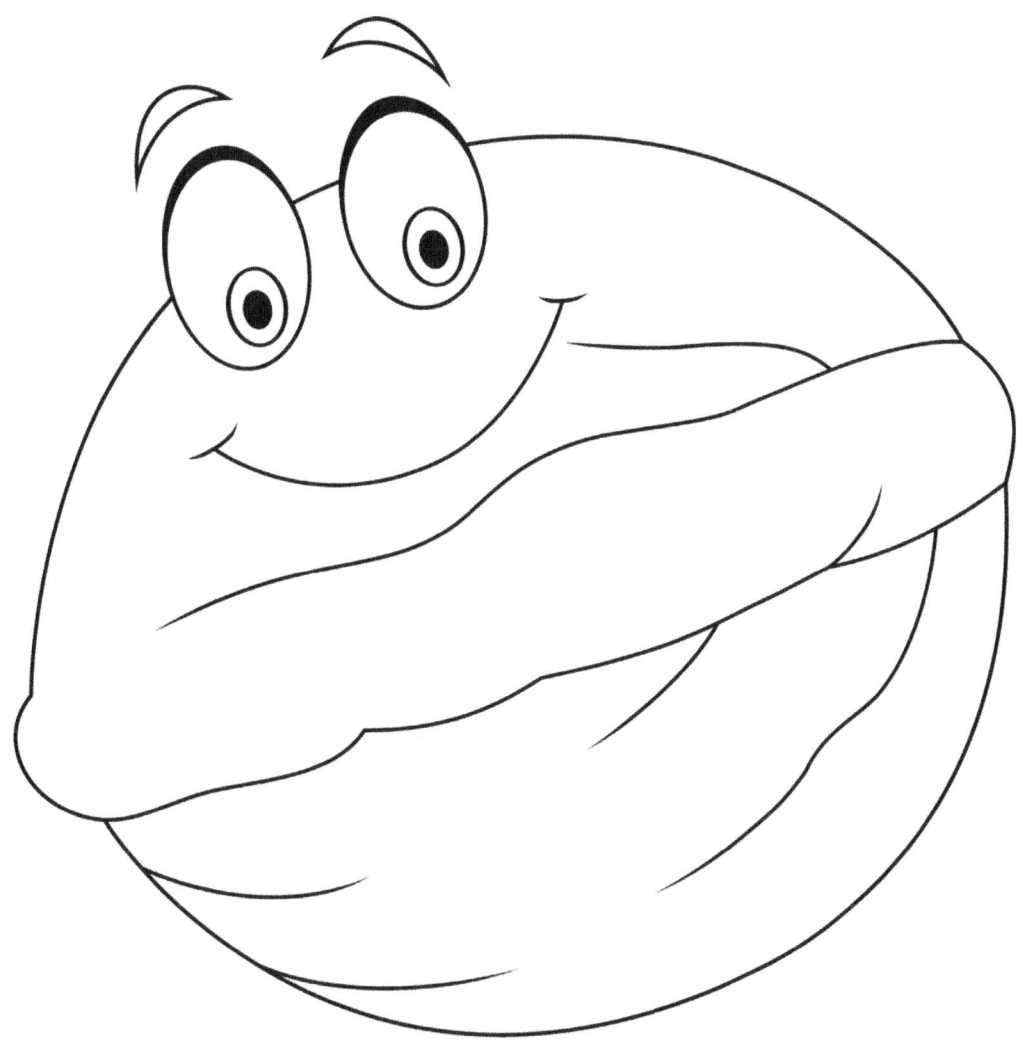

Nut

Nut

Krake

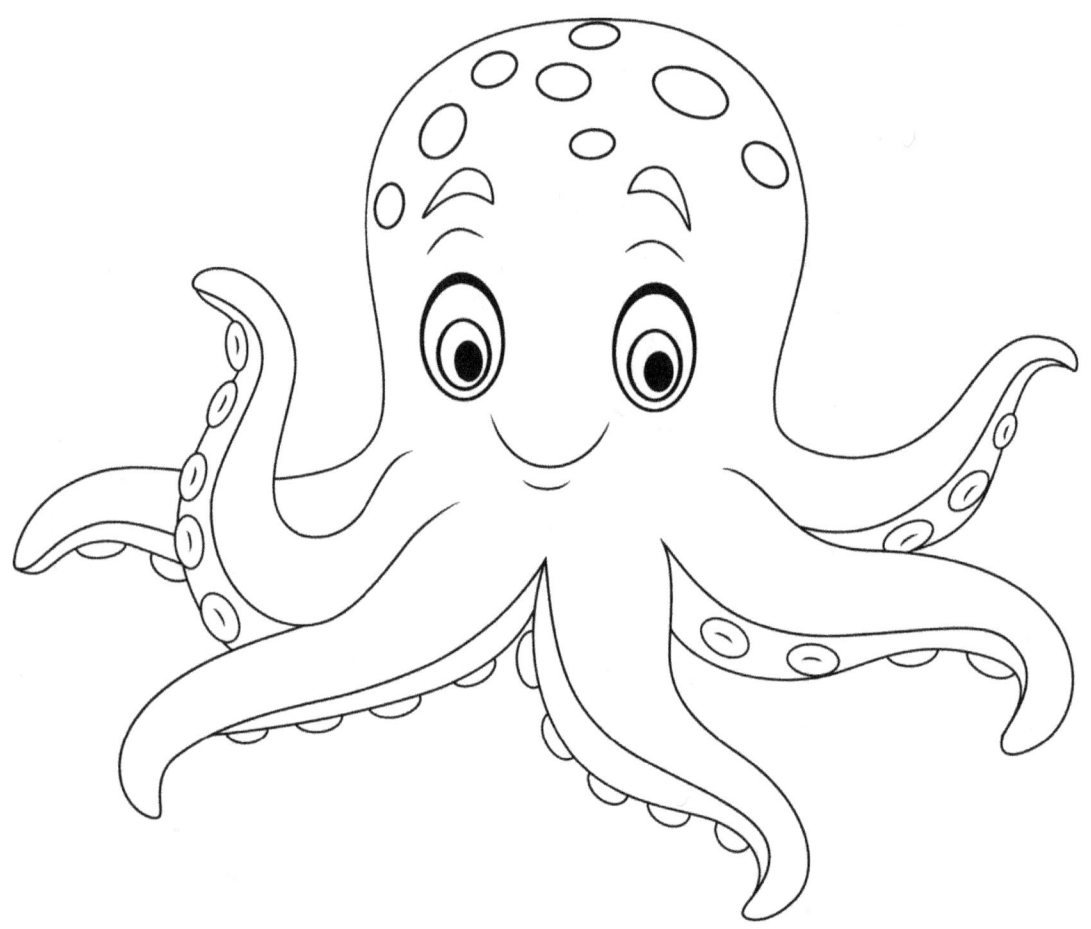

Octopus

Octopus

Orange

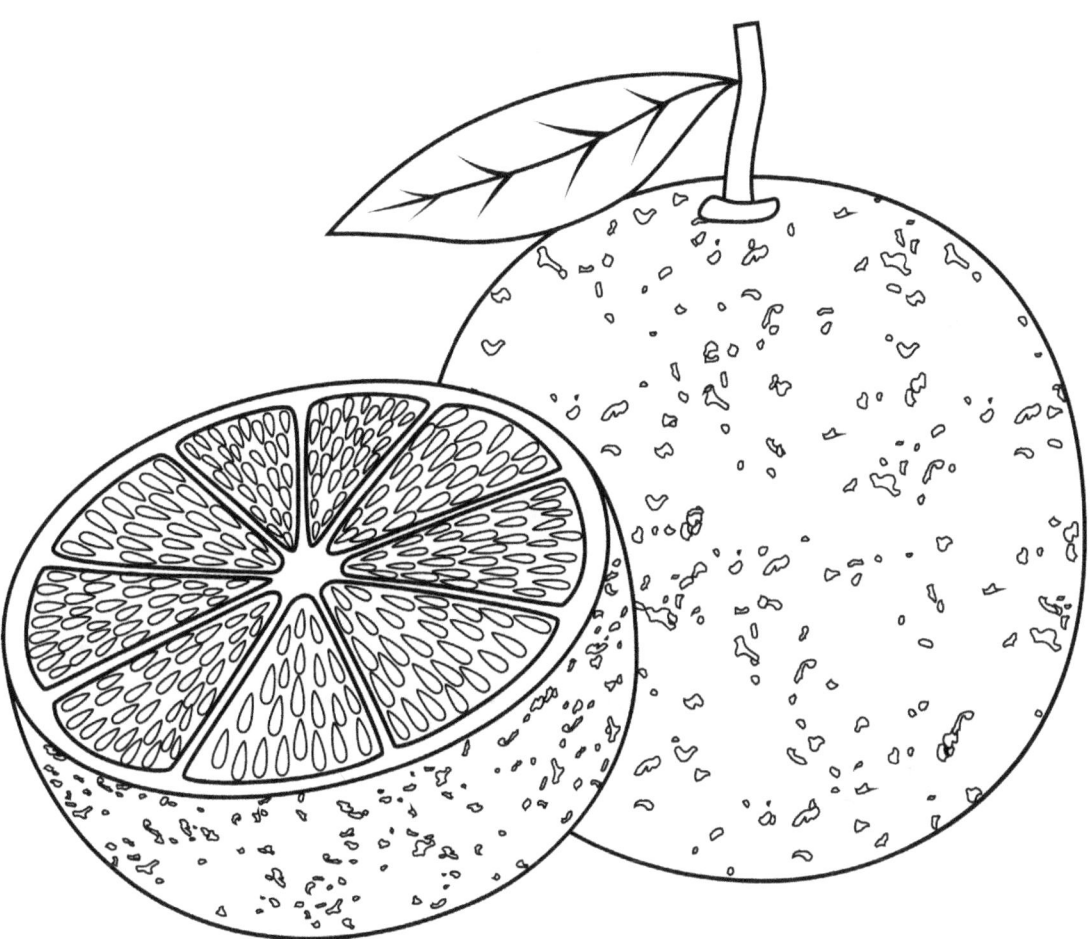

Orange

Orange

Pferd

Ho__e

Nuss

_u_

Krake

ctopu

Orange

Or__ge

Eule

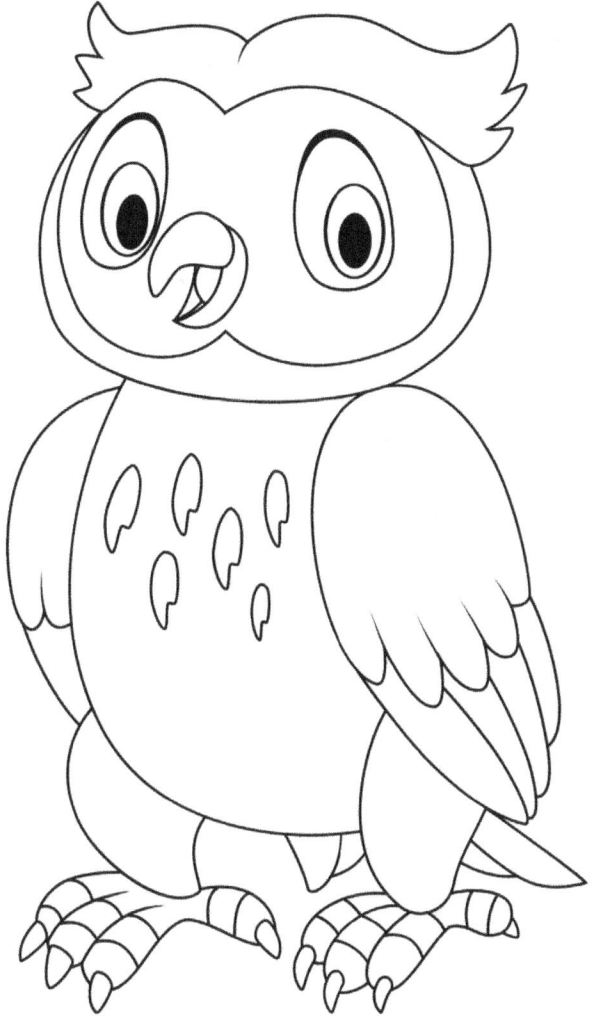

Owl

Owl

Stift

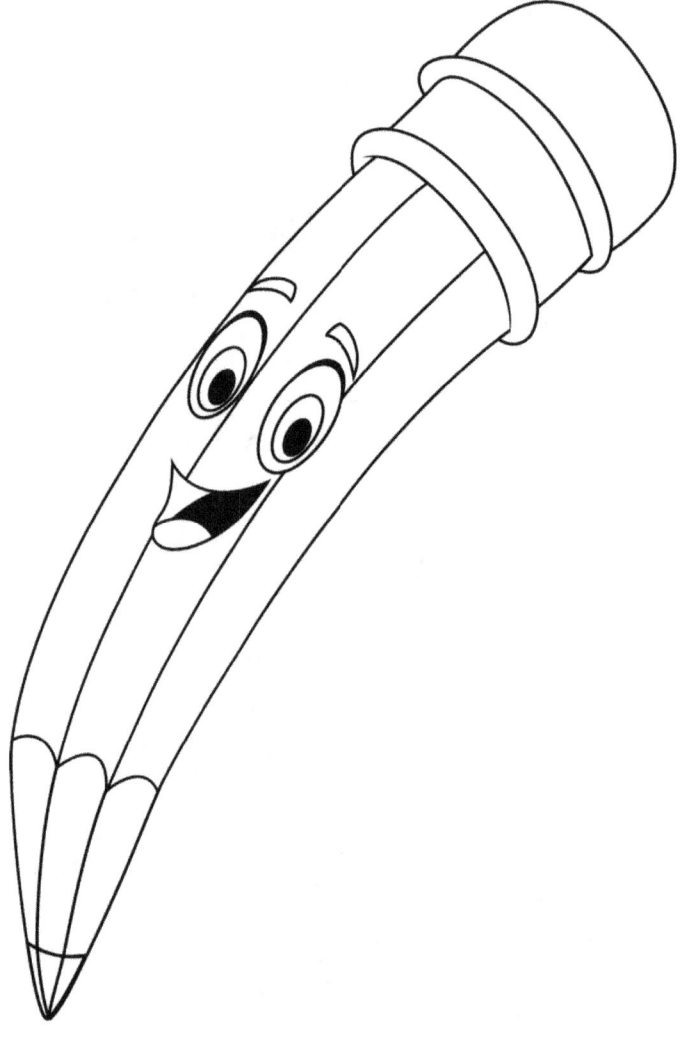

Pencil

Pencil
_____
_____
_____

Torte

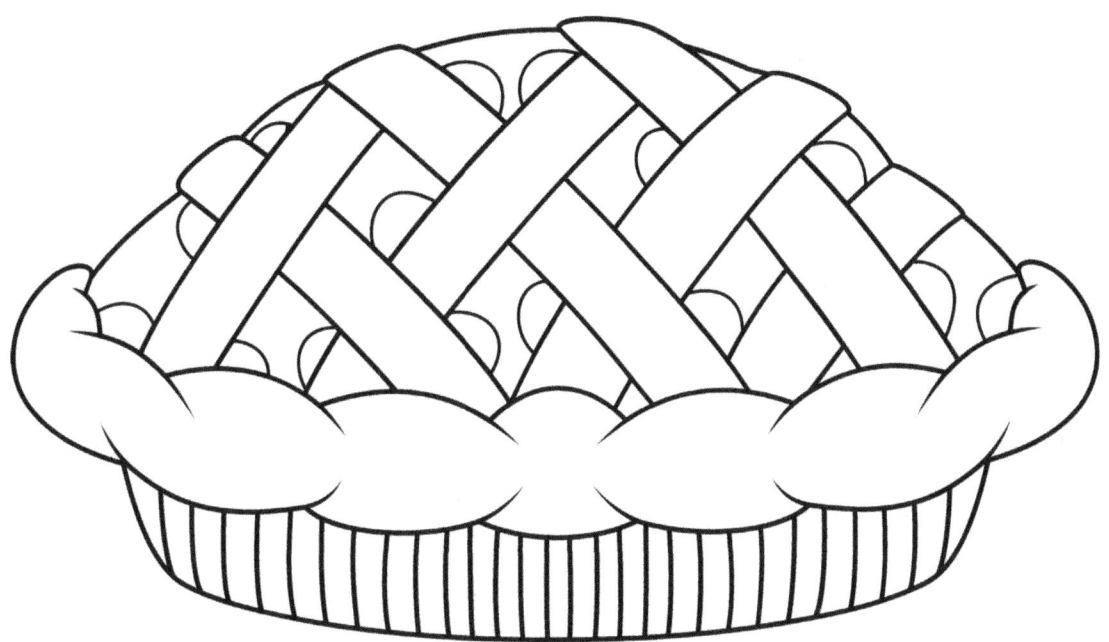

Pie

Pie
_____

_____

_____

Schwein

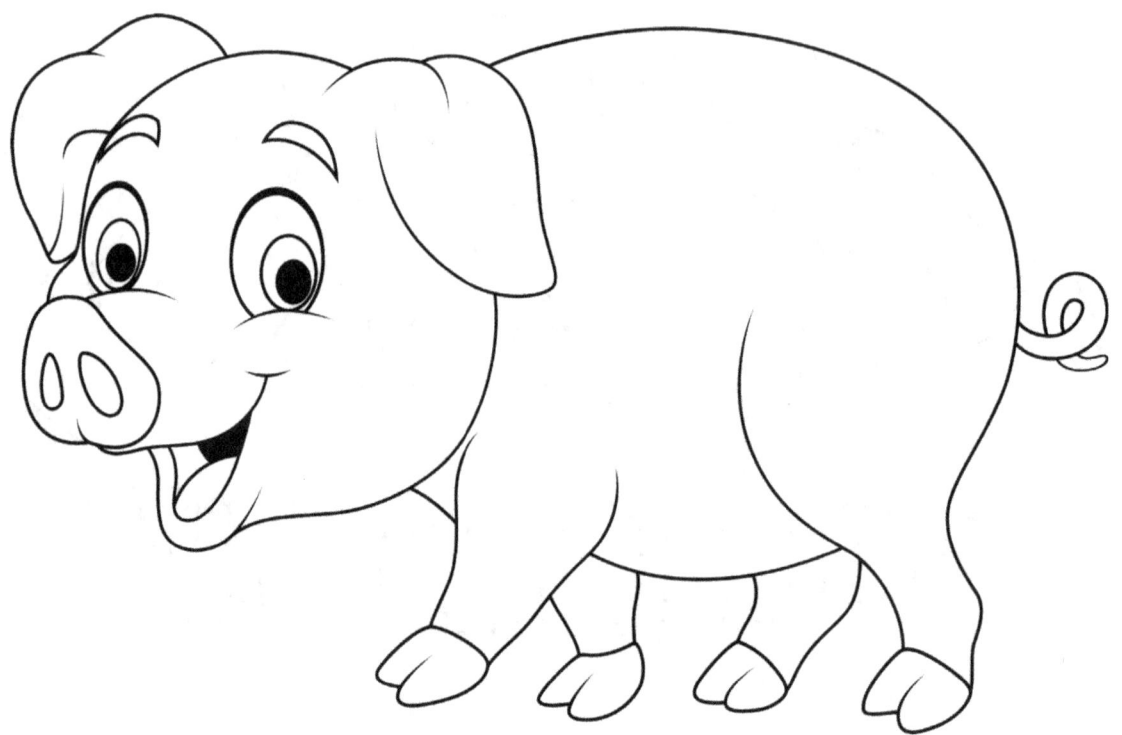

Pig

Pig
_____

_____

_____

Eule

o_l

Stift

_enc_l

Torte

__e

Schwein

__g

Vogel

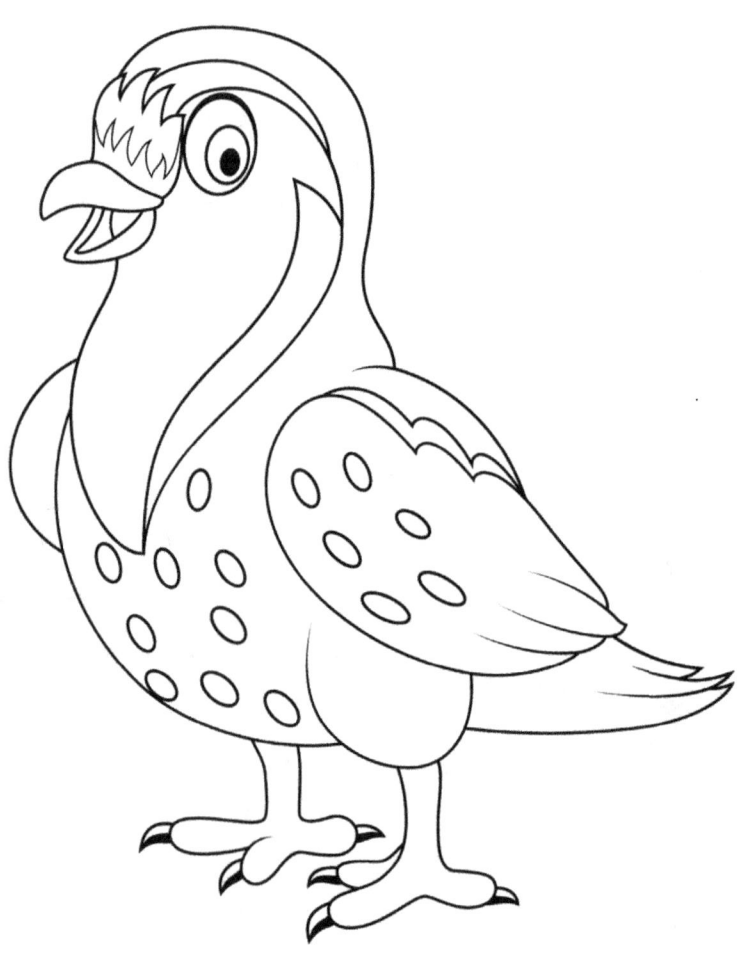

Bird

Bird

Königin

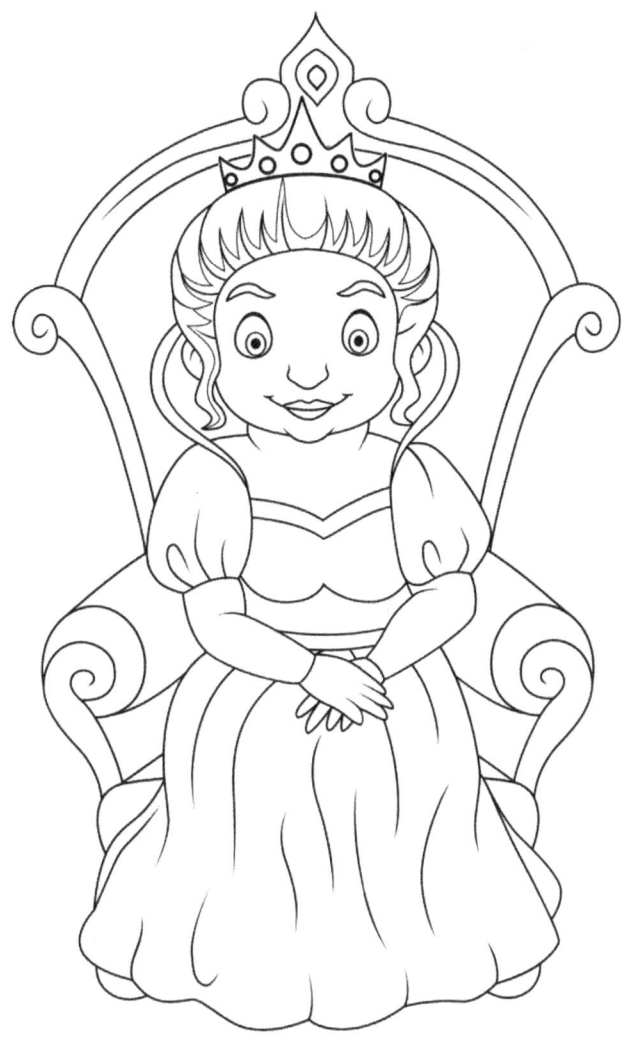

Queen

Queen

Feder

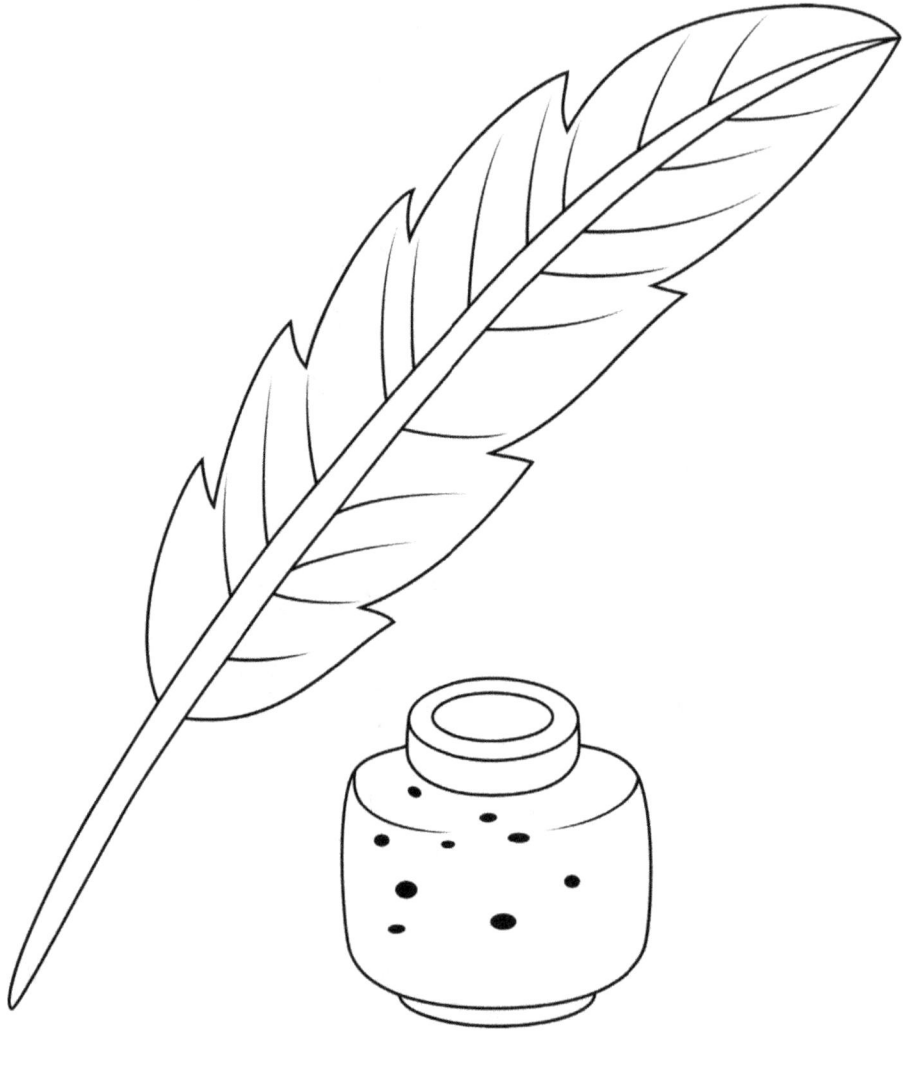

Quill

Quill

Hase

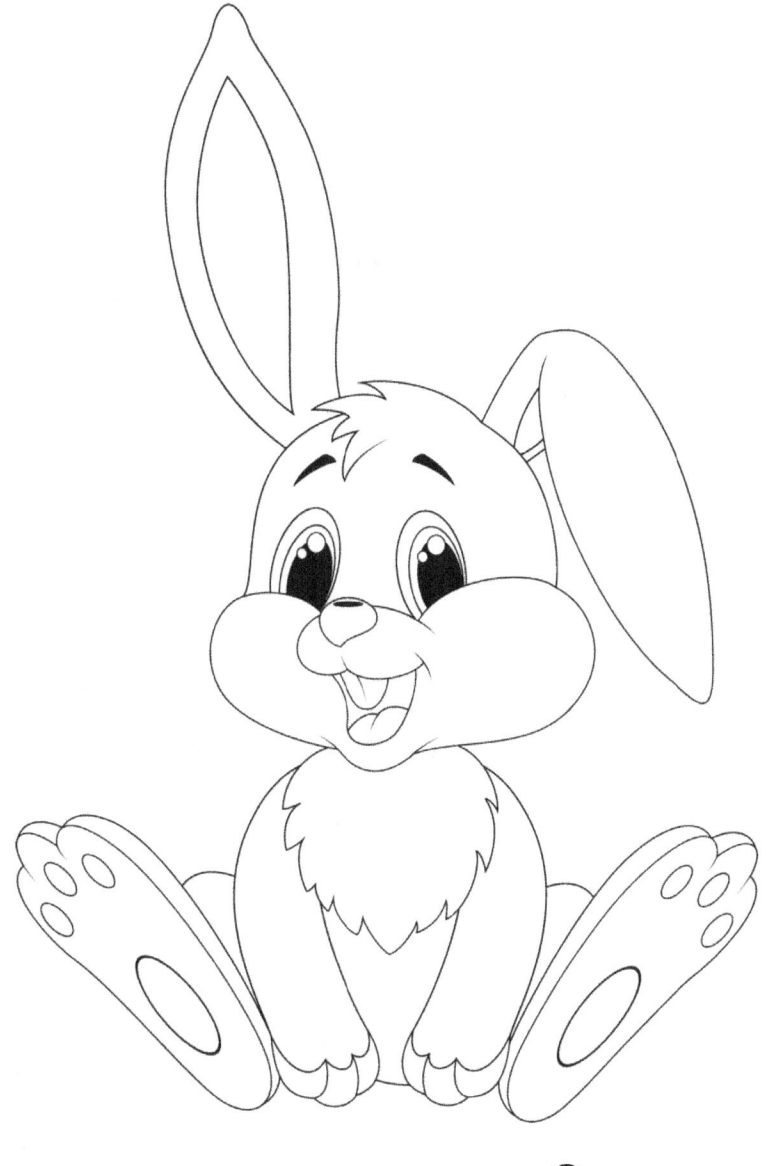

Rabbit

Rabbit

Vogel

Bi_d

Königin

_u_en

Feder

Q_i_l

Hase

Rab__t

Nashorn

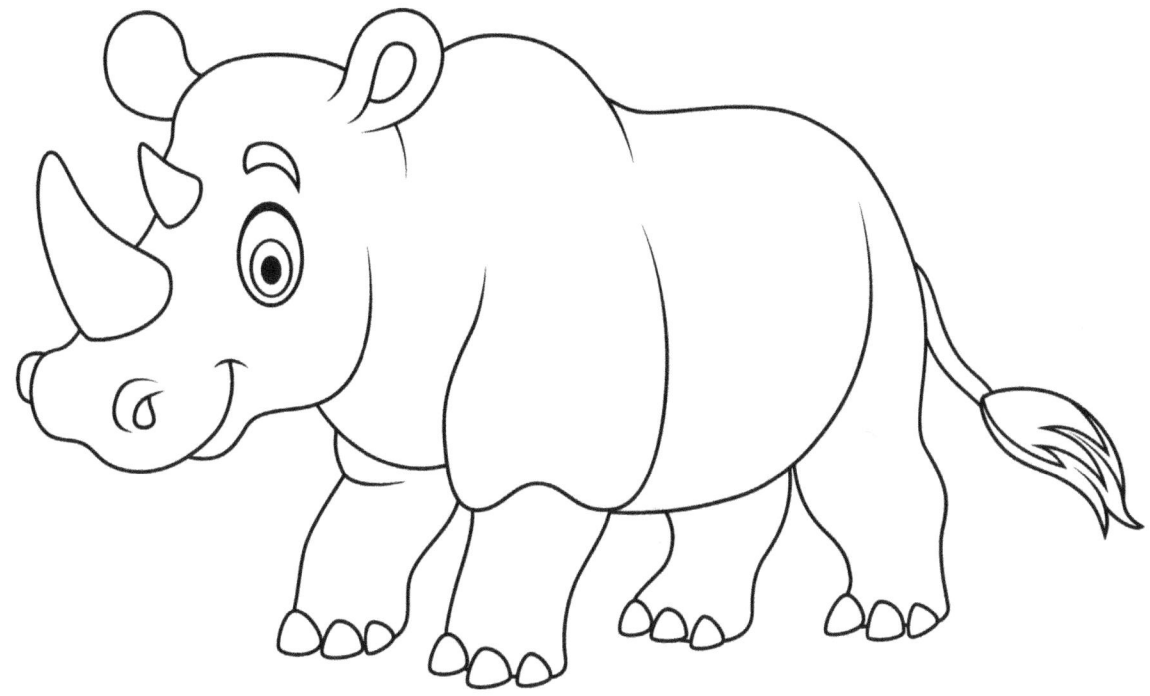

Rhino

Rhino

Roboter

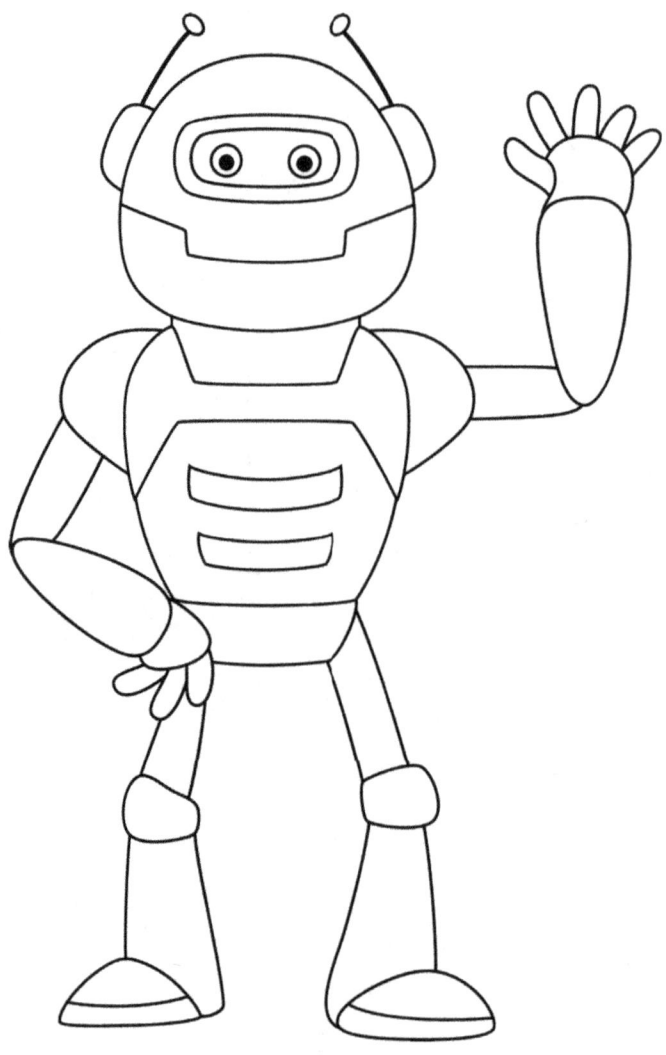

Robot

Robot
_____

_____

_____

Tiger

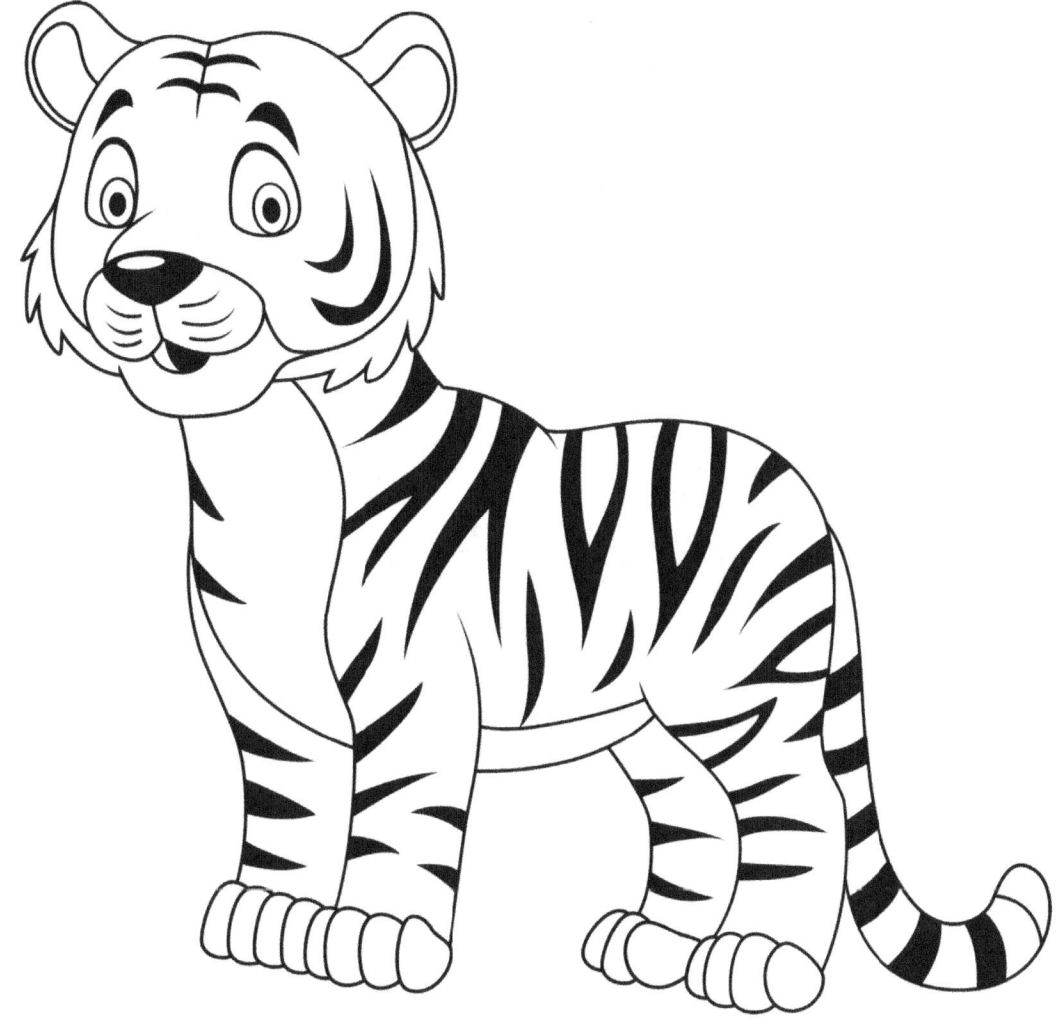

Tiger

Tiger
_____
_____
_____

Baum

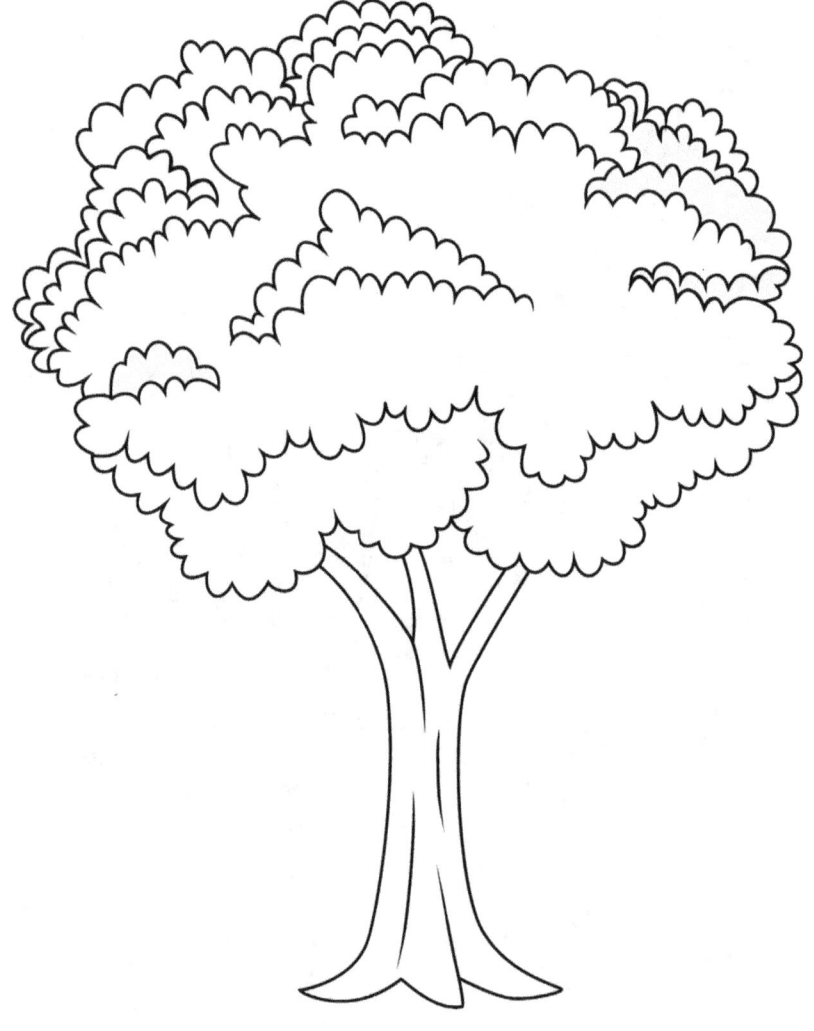

Tree

Tree

Nashorn

Rh__o

Roboter

_o_ot

Tiger

_i_er

Baum

Tr__

Regenschirm

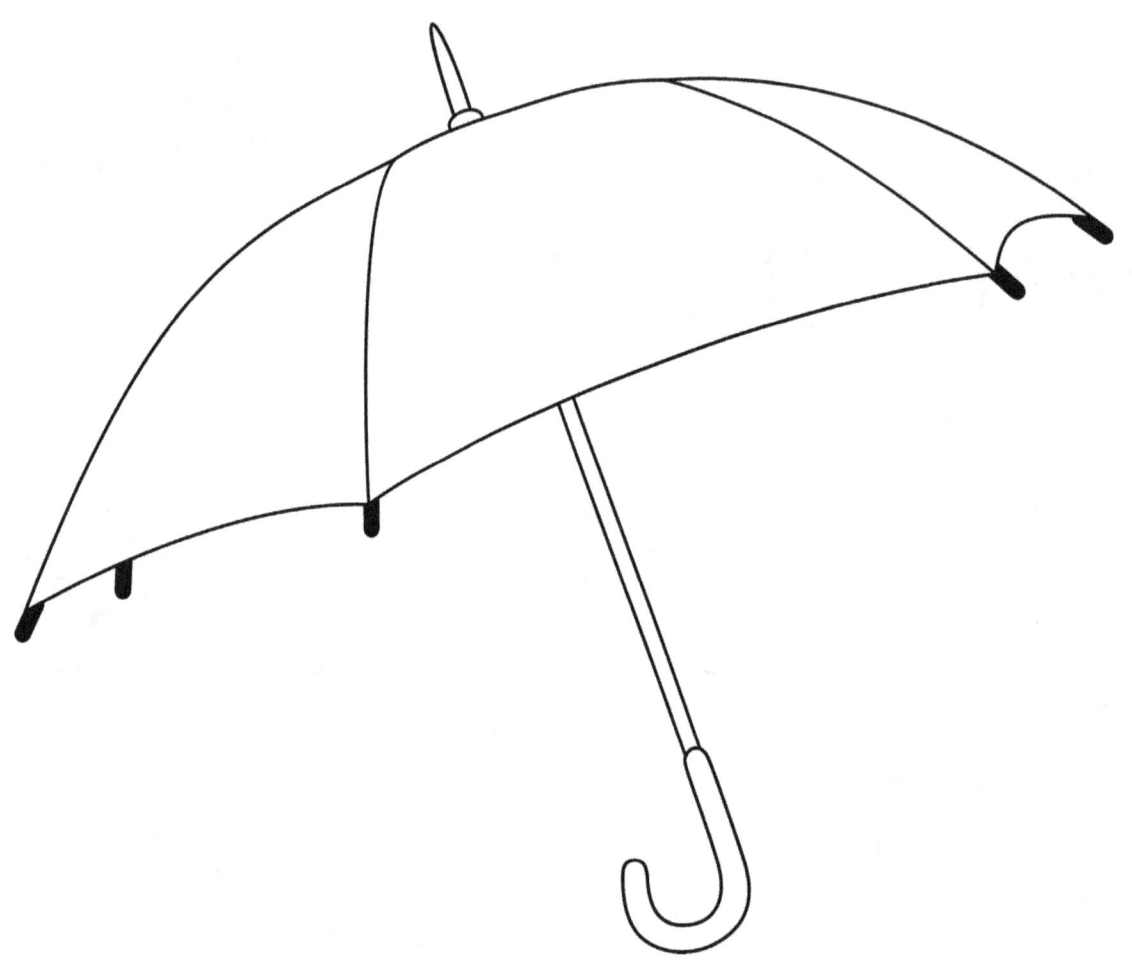

Umbrella

Umbrella

Seeigel

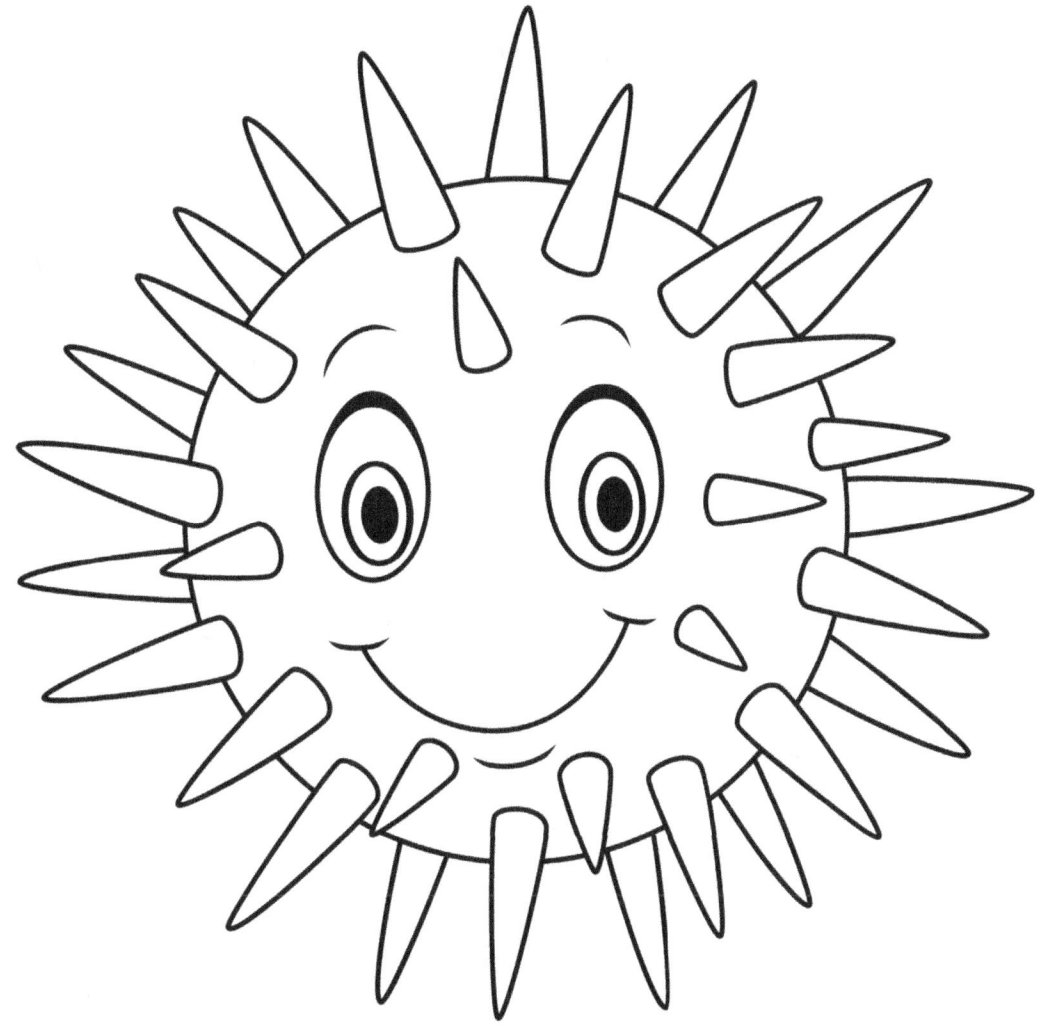

Urchin

Urchin

Sonne

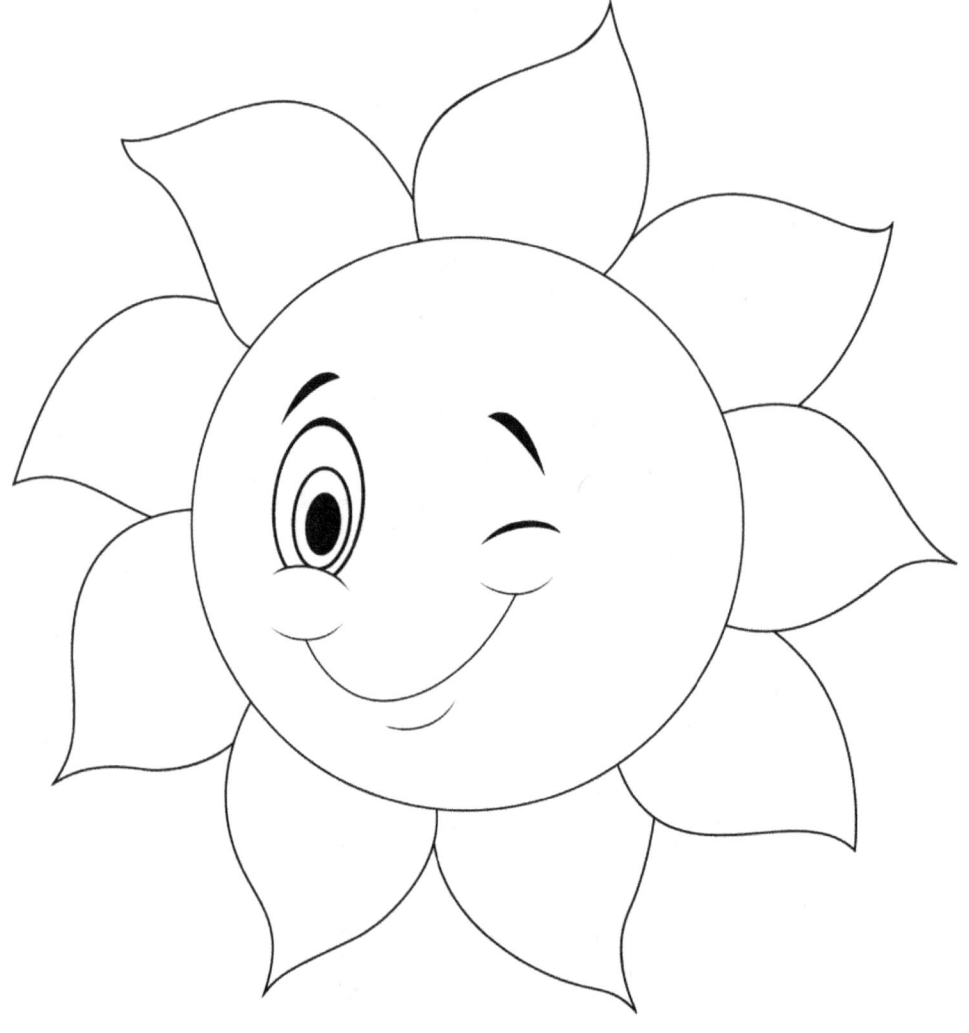

Sun

Sun
_____

_____

_____

Gemüse

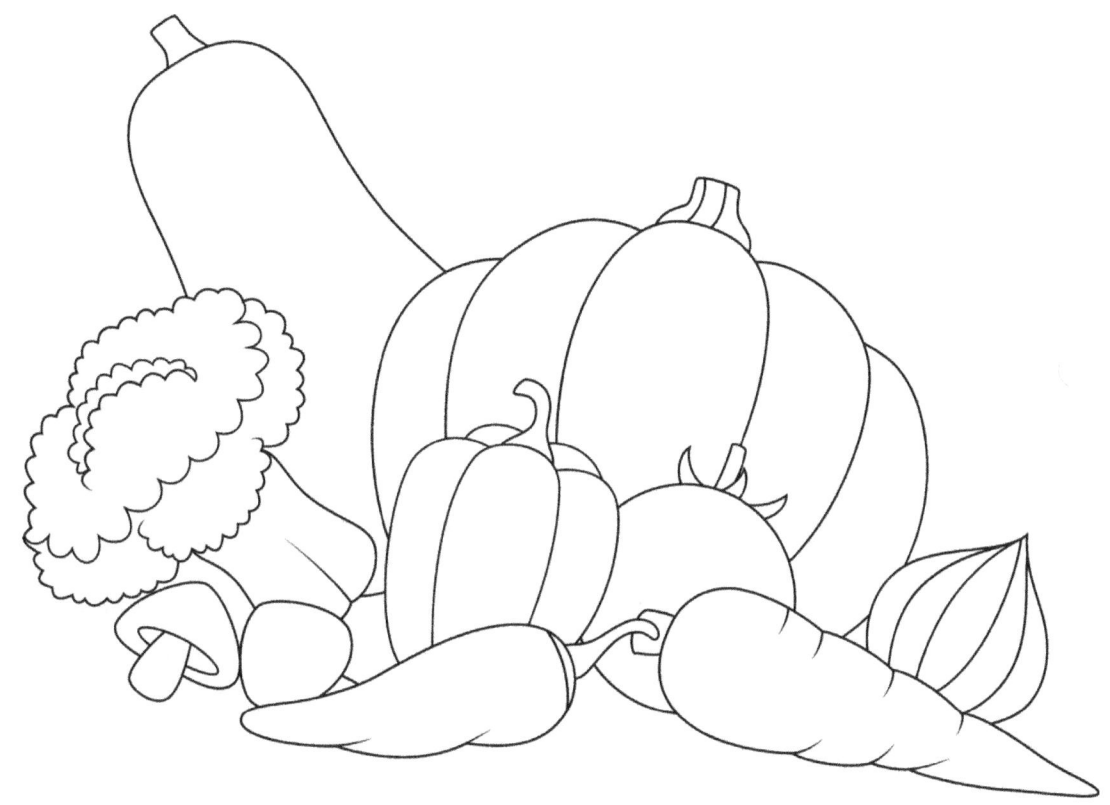

Vegetable

Vegetable
_____

_____

_____

Regenschirm

mbrell

Seeigel

_rc_in

Sonne

S__

Gemüse

Vegeta__e

Vulkan

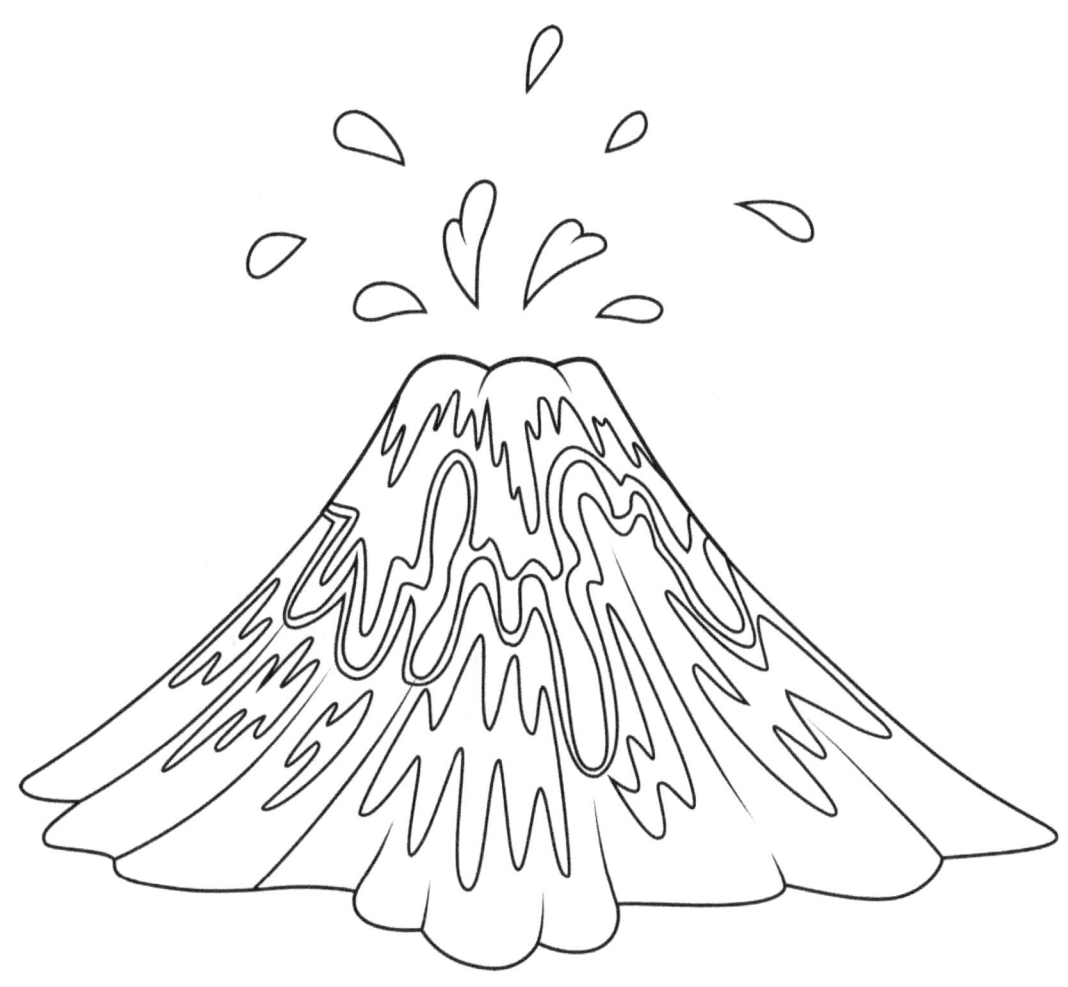

Volcano

Volcano

Geier

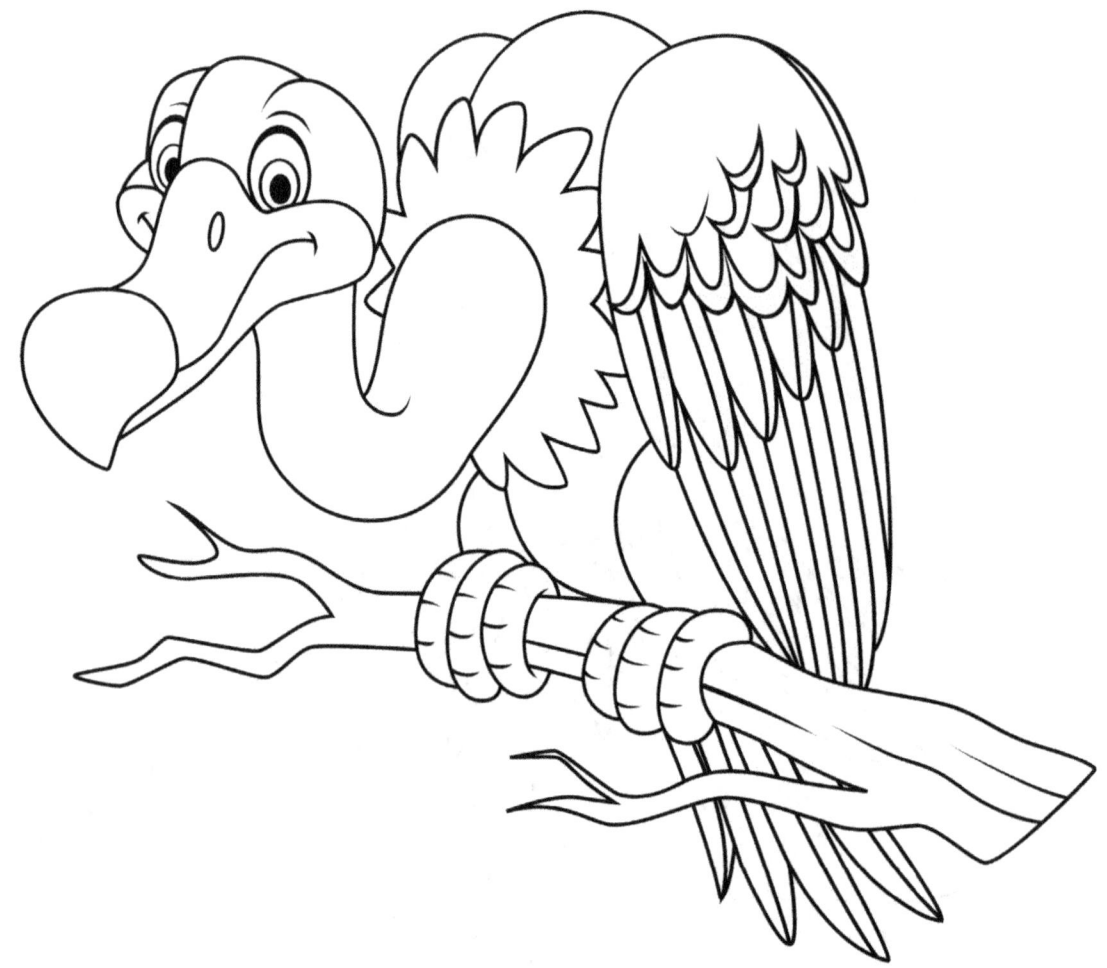

Vulture

Vulture

Wassermelone

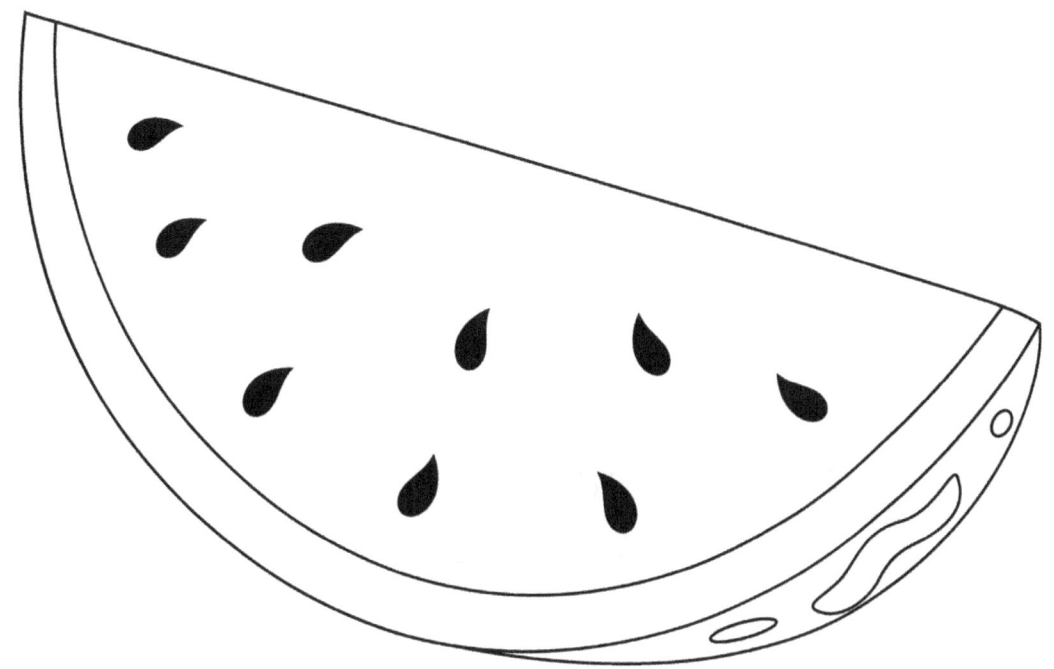

Watermelon

Watermelon

Wal

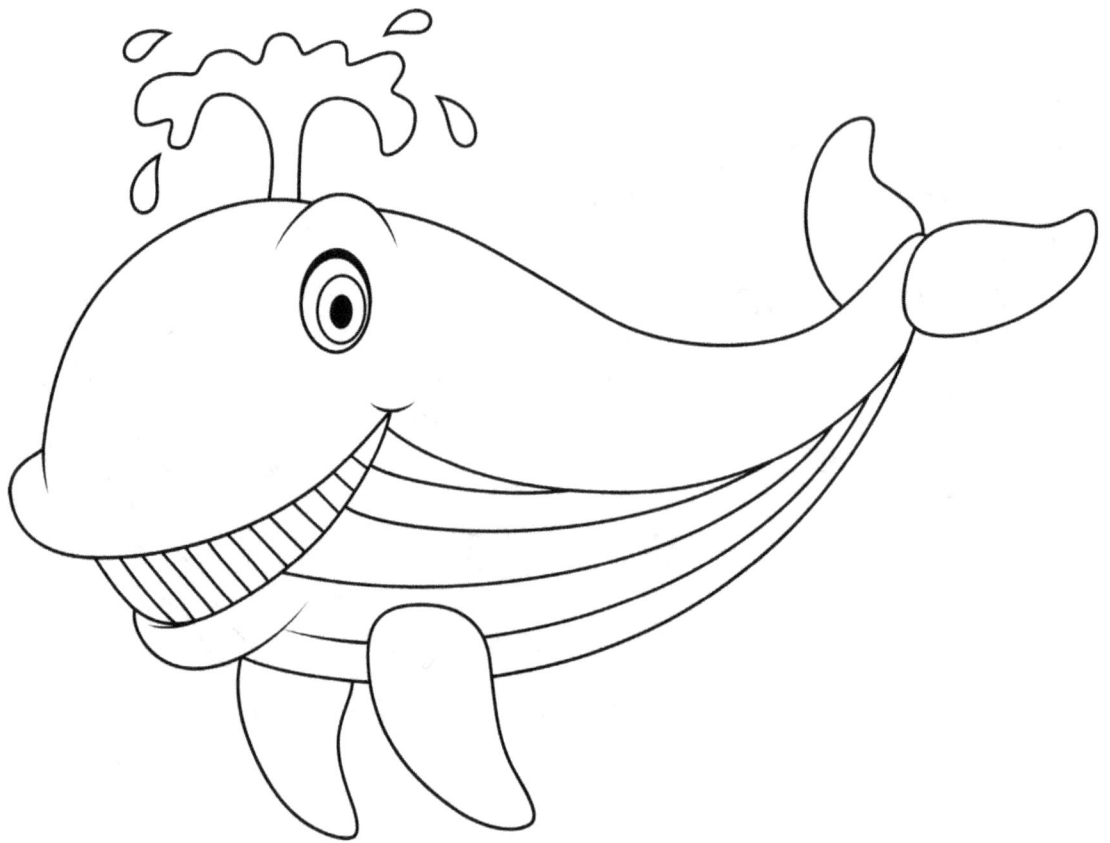

Whale

Whale
_____
_____
_____

Vulkan

Vo_c_no

Geier

Vu__ure

Wassermelone

Watermel__

Wal

__ale

Fenster

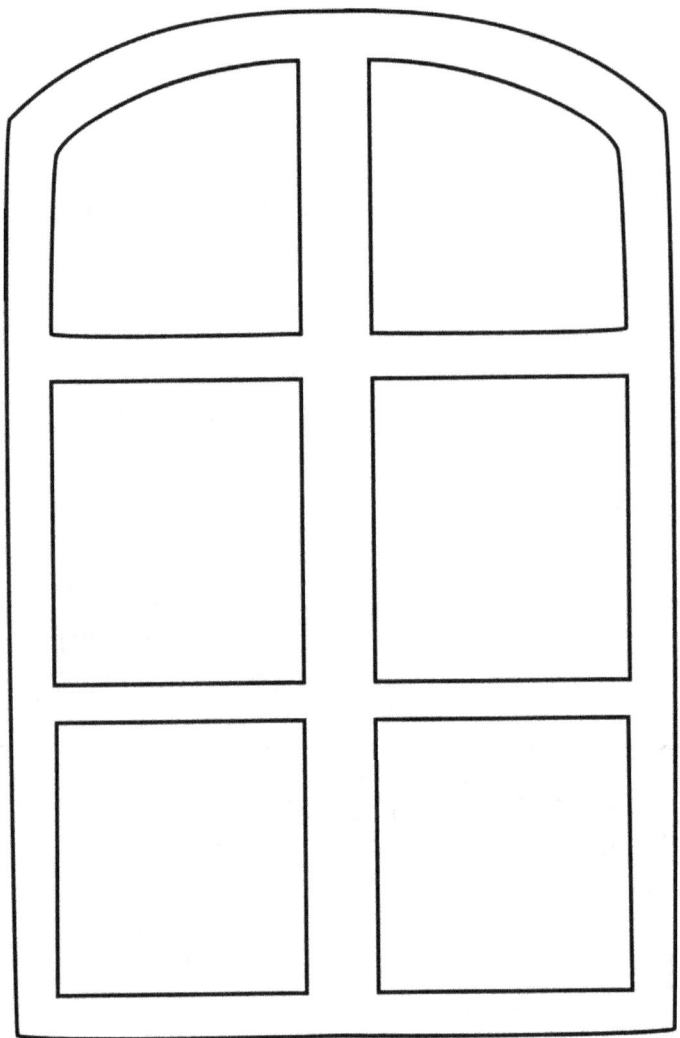

Window

Window

Xylophon

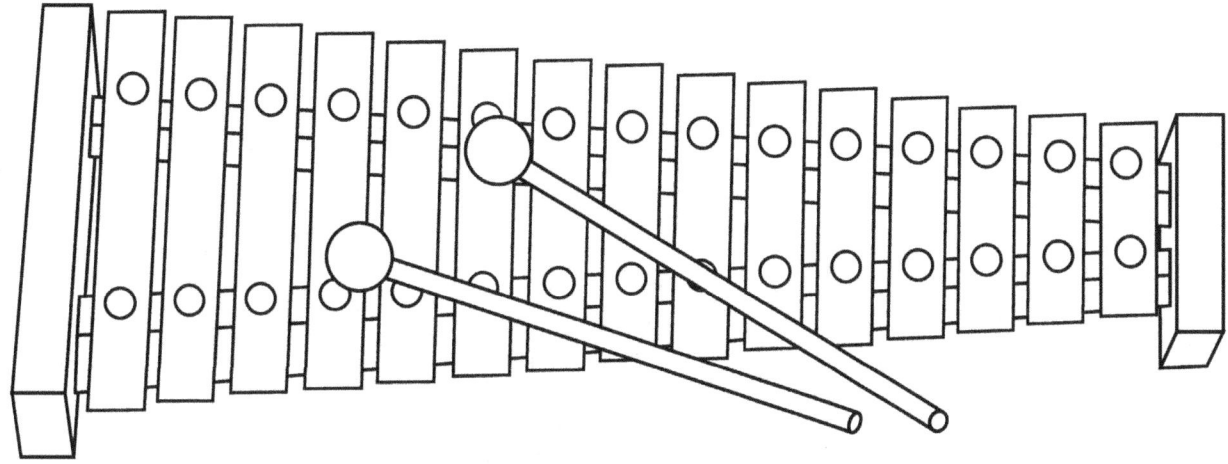

Xylophone

Xylophone

Segelschiff

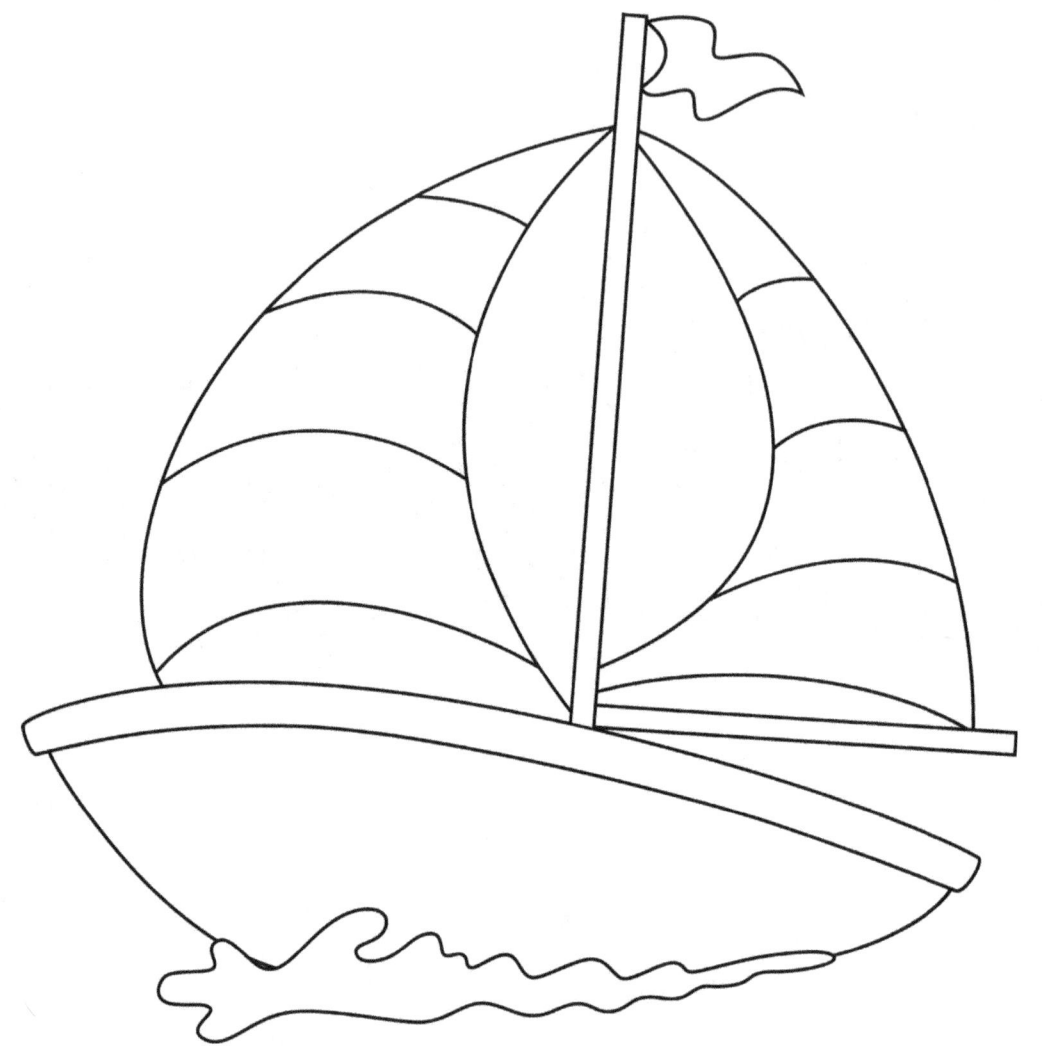

Sailing ship

Sailing ship

Schneemann

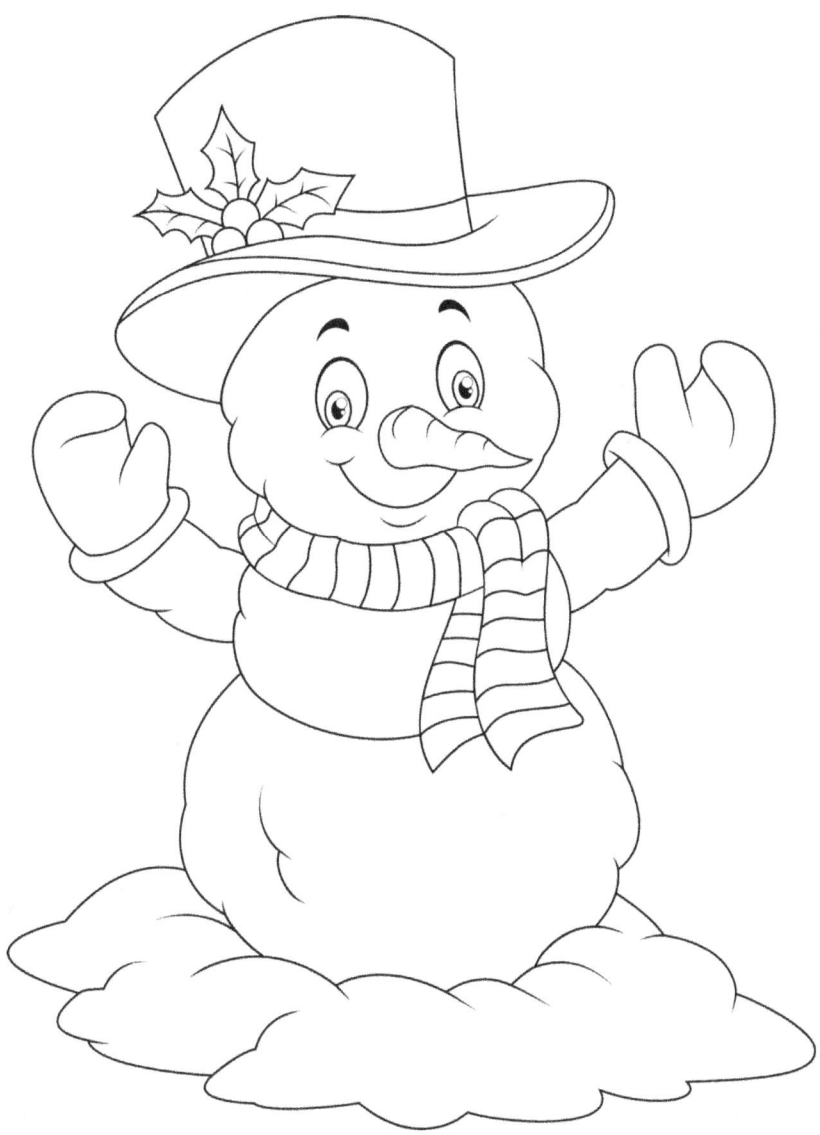

Snowman

Snowman

Fenster

W_ndo_

Xylophon

Xylo_h_ne

Segelschiff

S_ilin_ ship

Schneemann

S_owman

Joghurt

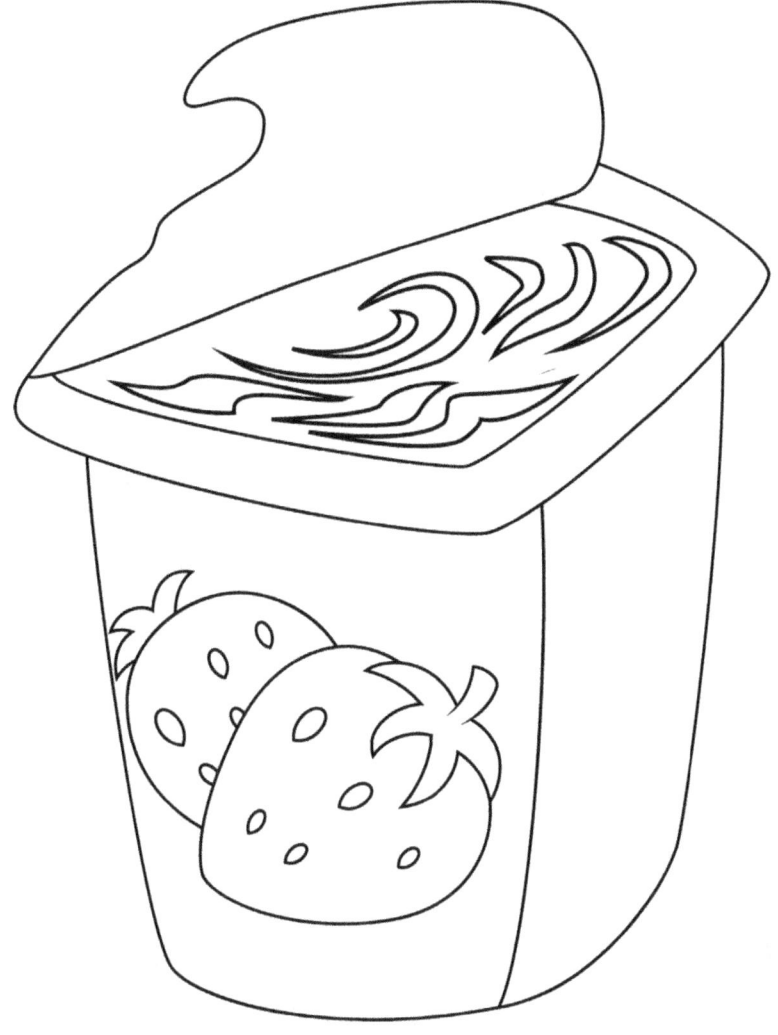

Yogurt

Yogurt

Huhn

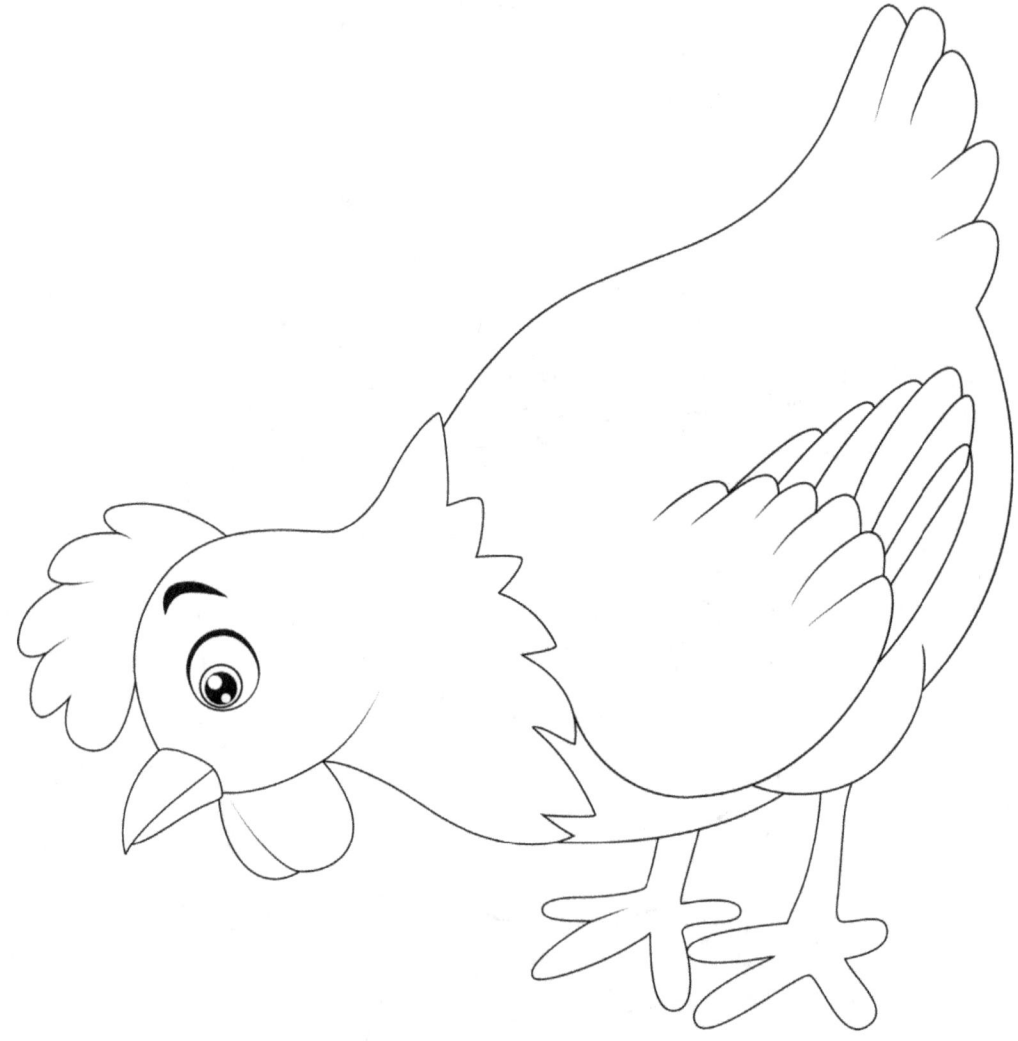

Chicken

Chicken

Schlüssel

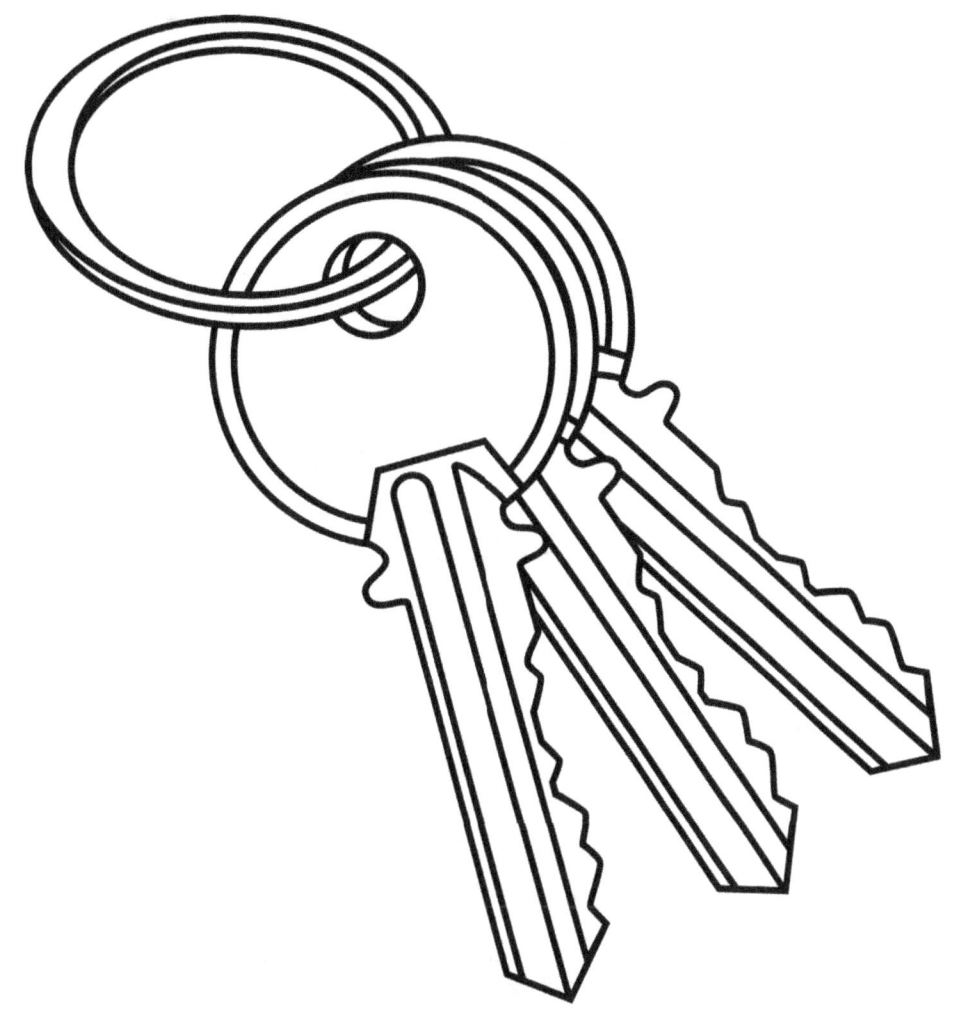

Key

Key _____

_____

_____

Koala

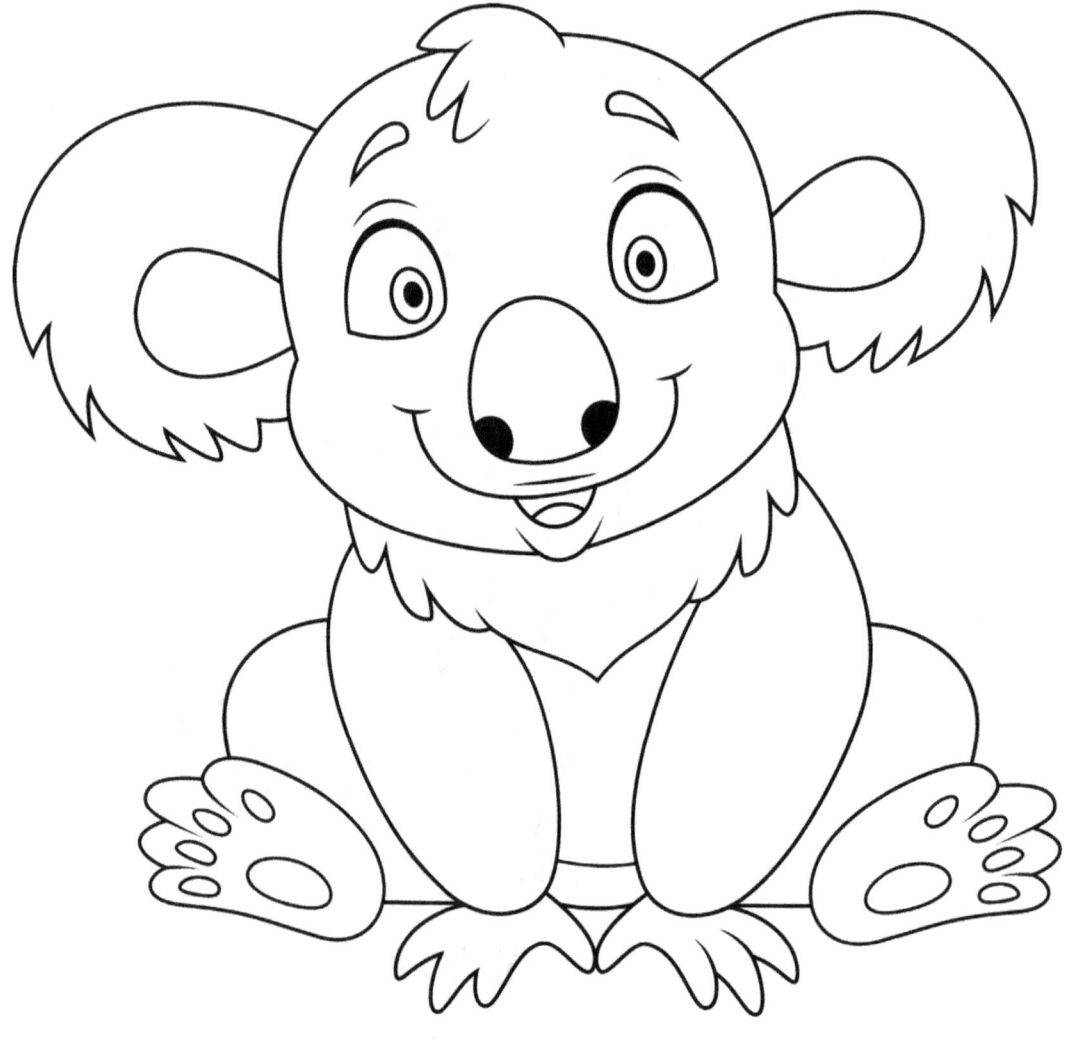

Koala

Koala

Joghurt

Yog__t

Huhn

C_ick_n

Schlüssel

K__

Koala

_oa_a

Ameise	-
Apfel	-
Raumfahrer	-
Banane	-
Bär	-
Buch	-
Auto	-
Katze	-
Mais	-
Hund	-
Donut	-
Trommel	-
Schnecke	-
Zebra	-
Elefant	-
Fisch	-

Blume	-
Fuchs	-
Giraffe	-
Brille	-
Weintrauben	-
Hamburger	-
Flusspferd	-
Haus	-
Eiscreme	-
Leguan	-
Ente	-
Jaguar	-
Marmelade	-
Qualle	-
Zeppelin	-
Kiwi	-
Erdbeere	-

Blätter	-
Lampe	-
Löwe	-
Affe	-
Maus	-
Fliegenpilz	-
Nagel	-
Pferd	-
Nuss	-
Krake	-
Orange	-
Eule	-
Stift	-
Torte	-
Schwein	-
Vogel	-
Königin	-

Feder	-
Hase	-
Nashorn	-
Roboter	-
Tiger	-
Baum	-
Regenschirm	-
Seeigel	-
Sonne	-
Gemüse	-
Vulkan	-
Geier	-
Wassermelone	-
Wal	-
Fenster	-
Xylophon	-
Segelschiff	-

Schneemann	-
Joghurt	-
Huhn	-
Schlüssel	-
Koala	-

© nerdMedia 2018

This work, including all its parts, is protected by copyright. Any use is not permitted without the author's consent. This applies in particular to copying, translation, storage and processing in electronic systems. Contact: Dirk Kolodziej/Peppermühl 9/48249 Dülmen/Germany info4us@nerdmedia.eu Cover design: nerdMedia Cover photo: depositphotos.com - Print Output Black & White: Amazon Media EU S.Ã .r.l./5 Rue Plaetis/L-2338 Luxembourg

www.ingramcontent.com/pod-product-compliance
Lightning Source LLC
Chambersburg PA
CBHW062332220526
45469CB00008B/2678